Richard Sw

Series Editor: Maria

The Merchant's Prologue & Tale

Geoffrey Chaucer

Philip Allan Updates
Market Place
Deddington
Oxfordshire
OX15 0SE
Tel: 01869 338652
Fax: 01869 337590
e-mail: sales@philipallan.co.uk
www.philipallan.co.uk

ISBN-13 978-1-84489-207-5
ISBN-10 1-84489-207-7

Printed by Raithby, Lawrence & Co Ltd, Leicester

Environmental information
The paper on which this title is printed is sourced from mills using wood from
managed, sustainable forests.

P00490

Contents

Introduction

Aims of the guide

The purpose of this Student Text Guide to 'The Merchant's Prologue and Tale' is to enable you to organise your thoughts and responses to the text, to deepen your understanding of key features and aspects, and finally to help you to address the particular requirements of examination questions in order to obtain the best possible grade. It will also prove useful to those writing a coursework piece on the text. The guide contains a number of summaries, lists, analyses and references to help with the content and construction of essay assignments. References to the text are to the Cambridge University Press edition, edited by Maurice Hussey.

It is assumed that you have read and studied the text already under the guidance of a teacher or lecturer. This is a revision guide, not an introduction, although some of its content serves the purpose of providing initial background. It can be read in its entirety in one sitting, or it can be dipped into and used as a reference guide to specific and separate aspects of the text.

The remainder of this Introduction section consists of exam board specifications and Assessment Objectives; a revision scheme which gives a suggested programme for using the material in the guide; and practical advice on writing essay answers.

The Text Guidance section consists of a series of subsections which examine key aspects of the text including contexts, interpretations and controversies. Emboldened terms within the Text Guidance section are glossed in 'literary terms and concepts' on pp. 57–61.

The final section, Questions and Answers, includes mark schemes, exemplar essay plans and examples of marked work.

Assessment Objectives

The Assessment Objectives (AOs) for A-level English Literature are common to all boards:

AO1	communicate clearly the knowledge, understanding and insight appropriate to literary study, using appropriate terminology and accurate and coherent written expression
AO2i	respond with knowledge and understanding to literary texts of different types and periods
AO2ii	respond with knowledge and understanding to literary texts of different types and periods, exploring and commenting on relationships and comparisons between literary texts

AO3	show detailed understanding of the ways in which writers' choices of form, structure and language shape meanings
AO4	articulate independent opinions and judgements, informed by different interpretations of literary texts by other readers
AO5i	show understanding of the contexts in which literary texts are written and understood
AO5ii	evaluate the significance of cultural, historical and other contextual influences on literary texts and study

A summary of each Assessment Objective is given below and would be worth memorising:

AO1	clarity of written communication
AO2	informed personal response in relation to time and genre (literary context)
AO3	the creative literary process (context of writing)
AO4	critical and interpretative response (context of reading)
AO5	evaluation of influences (cultural context)

It is essential that you pay close attention to the AOs, and their weighting, for the board for which you are entered. These are what the examiner will be looking for, and you must address them *directly* and *specifically*, in addition to proving general familiarity with and understanding of the text, and being able to present an argument clearly, relevantly and convincingly.

Remember that the examiners are seeking above all else evidence of an *informed personal response* to the text. A revision guide such as this can help you to understand the text and to form your own opinions, but it cannot replace your own ideas and responses as an individual reader.

Revision advice

For the examined units it is possible that either brief or more extensive revision will be necessary because the original study of the text took place some time previously. It is therefore useful to know how to go about revising and which tried and tested methods are considered the most successful for literature exams at all levels, from GCSE to degree finals.

Below is a guide on how not to do it — think of reasons why not in each case.

Don't:
- leave it until the last minute
- assume you remember the text well enough and don't need to revise at all

- spend hours designing a beautiful revision schedule
- revise more than one text at the same time
- think you don't need to revise because it is an open book exam
- decide in advance what you think the questions will be and revise only for those
- try to memorise particular essay plans
- reread texts randomly and aimlessly
- revise for longer than 2 hours in one sitting
- miss school lessons in order to work alone at home
- try to learn a whole ring-binder's worth of work
- rely on a study guide instead of the text

There are no short-cuts to effective exam revision; the only one way to know a text well, and to know your way around it in an exam, is to have done the necessary studying. If you use the following method, in six easy stages, for both open and closed book revision, you will not only revisit and reassess all your previous work on the text in a manageable way but will be able to distil, organise and retain your knowledge. Don't try to do it all in one go: take regular breaks for refreshment and a change of scene.

(1) Between a month and a fortnight before the exam, depending on your schedule (a simple list of stages with dates displayed in your room, not a work of art!), you will need to reread the text, this time taking stock of all the underlinings and marginal annotations as well. As you read, collect onto sheets of A4 the essential ideas and quotations as you come across them. The acts of selecting key material and recording it as notes are natural ways of stimulating thought and aiding memory.

(2) Reread the highlighted areas and marginal annotations in your critical extracts and background handouts, and add anything useful from them to your list of notes and quotations. Then reread your previous essays and the teacher's comments. As you look back through essays written earlier in the course, you should have the pleasant sensation of realising that you can now write much better on the text than you could then. You will also discover that much of your huge file of notes is redundant or repeated, and that you have changed your mind about some beliefs, so that the distillation process is not too daunting. Selecting what is important is the way to crystallise your knowledge and understanding.

(3) During the run-up to the exam you need to do lots of practice essay plans to help you identify any gaps in your knowledge and give you practice in planning in 5–8 minutes. Past paper titles for you to plan are provided in this guide, some of which can be done as full timed essays — and marked strictly according to exam criteria — which will show whether length and timing are problematic for you. If you have not seen a copy of a real exam paper before you take your first module, ask to see a past paper so that you are familiar with the layout and rubric.

(4) About a week before the exam, reduce your two or three sides of A4 notes to a double-sided postcard of very small, dense writing. Collect a group of keywords by once again selecting and condensing, and use abbreviations for quotations (first and last word), and character and place names (initials). (For the comparison unit your postcard will need to refer to key points, themes and quotations in both texts relevant to the specific theme or genre topic.) The act of choosing and writing out the short quotations will help you to focus on the essential issues, and to recall them quickly in the exam. Make sure that your selection covers the main themes and includes examples of symbolism, style, comments on character, examples of irony, point of view or other significant aspects of the text. Previous class discussion and essay writing will have indicated which quotations are useful for almost any title; pick those which can serve more than one purpose, for instance those which reveal character and theme, and are also an example of language. In this way a minimum number of quotations can have maximum application.

(5) You now have in a compact, accessible form all the material for any possible essay title. There are only half a dozen themes relevant to a literary text so if you have covered these, you should not meet with any nasty surprises when you read the exam questions. You don't need to refer to your file of paperwork again, or even to the text. For the few days before the exam, you can read through your handy postcard whenever and wherever you get the opportunity. Each time you read it, which will only take a few minutes, you are reminding yourself of all the information you will be able to recall in the exam to adapt to the general title or to support an analysis of particular passages.

(6) A fresh, active mind works wonders, and information needs time to settle, so don't try to cram just before the exam. Relax the night before and get a good night's sleep. Then you will be able to enter the exam room with all the confidence of a well-prepared candidate.

Writing examination essays

Essay content

One of the key skills you are being asked to demonstrate at A-level is the ability to select and tailor your knowledge of the text and its background to the question set in the exam paper. In order to reach the highest levels, you need to avoid 'pre-packaged' essays which lack focus, relevance and coherence, and which simply contain everything you know about the text. Be ruthless in rejecting irrelevant material, after considering whether it can be made relevant by a change of emphasis. Aim to cover the whole question, not just part of it; your response needs to demonstrate breadth and depth, covering the full range of text elements: character, event, theme and language. Only half a dozen approaches are possible for any set text, though they may be phrased in a variety of ways, and they are likely to refer to the key themes of the text. Preparation of the text therefore involves extensive discussion and practice at manipulating these core themes so that there should be no surprises in the exam. An apparently new angle is more likely to be something familiar presented in an unfamiliar way and you should not panic or reject the choice of question because you think you know nothing about it.

Exam titles are open-ended in the sense that there is not an obvious right answer, and you would therefore be unwise to give a dismissive, extreme or entirely one-sided response. The question would not have been set if the answer were not debatable. An ability and willingness to see both sides is an Assessment Objective and shows independence of judgement as a reader. Don't be afraid to explore the issues and don't try to tie the text into one neat interpretation. If there is ambiguity, it is likely to be deliberate on the part of the author and must be discussed; literary texts are complex and often paradoxical, and it would be a misreading of them to suggest that there is only one possible interpretation. You are not expected, however, to argue equally strongly or extensively for both sides of an argument, since personal opinion is an important factor. It is advisable to deal with the alternative view at the beginning of your response, and then construct your own view as the main part of the essay. This makes it less likely that you will appear to cancel out your own line of argument.

Choosing the right question

The first skill you must show when presented with the exam paper is the ability to choose the better, for you, of the two questions on your text where there is a choice. This is not to say that you should always go for the same type of essay (whole-text or poem-based), and if the question is not one which you feel happy with for any reason, you should seriously consider the other, even if it is not the type you normally prefer. It is unlikely but possible that a question contains a word you are not sure you know the meaning of, in which case it would be safer to choose the other one.

Don't be tempted to choose a question because of its similarity to one you have already done. Freshness and thinking on the spot usually produce a better product than attempted recall of a previous essay which may have received only a mediocre mark in the first place. The exam question is unlikely to have exactly the same focus and your response may seem 'off centre' as a result, as well as stale and perfunctory in expression. Essay questions fall into the following categories: close section analysis and relation to whole text; characterisation; setting and atmosphere; structure and effectiveness; genre;

language and style; themes and issues. Remember, however, that themes are relevant to all essays and that analysis, not just description, is always required.

Once you have decided which exam question to attempt, follow the procedure below for whole-text and passage-based, open- and closed-book essays.

(1) Underline all the key words in the question and note how many parts the question has.

(2) Plan your answer, using aspects of the key words and parts of the question as sub-headings, in addition to themes. Aim for 10–12 ideas. Check that the Assessment Objectives are covered.

(3) Support your argument by selecting the best examples of characters, events, imagery and quotations to prove your points. Remove ideas for which you can find no evidence.

(4) Structure your answer by grouping and numbering your points in a logical progression. Identify the best general point to keep for the conclusion.

(5) Introduce your essay with a short paragraph setting the context and defining the key words in the question as broadly, but relevantly, as possible.

(6) Write the rest of the essay, following your structured plan but adding extra material if it occurs to you. Paragraph your writing and consider expression, especially sentence structure and vocabulary choices, as you write. Signal changes in the direction of your argument with paragraph openers such as 'Furthermore' and 'However'. Use plenty of short, integrated quotations and use the words of the text rather than your own where possible. Use technical terms appropriately, and write concisely and precisely, avoiding vagueness and ambiguity.

(7) Your conclusion should sound conclusive and make it clear that you have answered the question. It should be an overview of the question and the text, not a repetition or a summary of points already made.

(8) Cross out your plan with a neat, diagonal line.

(9) Check your essay for content, style, clarity and accuracy. With neat crossings-out, correct errors of fact, spelling, grammar and punctuation. Improve expression if possible, and remove any repetition and irrelevance. Add clarification and missing evidence, if necessary, using omission marks or asterisks. Even at this stage, good new material can be added.

There is no such thing as a perfect or model essay; flawed essays can gain full marks. There is always something more which could have been said, and examiners realise that students have limitations when writing under pressure in timed conditions. You are not penalised for what you didn't say in comparison to some idealised concept of the answer, but rewarded for the knowledge and understanding you have shown. It is not as difficult as you may think to do well, provided that you are familiar with the text and have sufficient essay-writing experience. If you follow the above process and **underline, plan, support, structure, write** and **check**, you can't go far wrong.

Text Guidance

Contexts

This guide is designed to help you make sense of 'The Merchant's Prologue and Tale' both in relation to its parent work, *The Canterbury Tales*, and in its historical and cultural context. For this reason, reference is made throughout the guide to *The Canterbury Tales* as a whole and to 'The General Prologue' in particular, which you should read in detail as background to 'The Merchant's Prologue and Tale'.

Assessment Objective 5 requires the candidate to 'evaluate the significance of cultural, historical and other contextual influences on literary texts'. There are a number of contexts in which 'The Merchant's Prologue and Tale' can be viewed.

Chaucer's life

Although nothing is known about Chaucer as a person, and almost nothing about his private life, he was a prominent figure in the second half of the fourteenth century, with associations and positions at court. He served under three kings, and was entrusted by Edward III with foreign journeys handling the king's secret affairs. The public aspects of his life are therefore well documented, and demonstrate that he would have had direct experience of nearly all the kinds of people he represents in *The Canterbury Tales*.

There are some uncertainties and some periods of Chaucer's life for which little is known, but the salient dates are outlined below. The approximate dates for the composition of his literary works are also given.

Key dates and works

c. 1340–45	Geoffrey Chaucer born, son of a London wine merchant.
1357	Becomes a page in the household of the Countess of Ulster.
1360	Captured while serving in France; ransomed by Edward III.
1366	Journeys to Spain; marries Philippa Rouet around this time.
1367	Appointed Yeoman of the Chamber in the king's household.
1367–77	Journeys abroad on the king's business.
1369	Campaigns in France; appointed Esquire in the king's household.
Pre-1372	*The Book of the Duchess*.
1372–73	First journey to Italy.
1372–80	*The House of Fame*.
1374	Appointed Comptroller of Customs and Subsidy.
1377	Edward III dies; accession of Richard II.
1378	Second journey to Italy.
1380–86	*The Parliament of Fowls; Troilus and Criseyde; The Legend of Good Women*.

1385	Appointed Justice of the Peace for Kent.
1385–1400	*The Canterbury Tales.*
1386	Sits in Parliament as Knight of the Shire for Kent.
1389	Appointed Clerk to the King's Works.
1391	Appointed Subforester.
1394	Awarded extra grant for good service.
1399	Richard II deposed; accession of Henry IV.
	Previous grants confirmed by Henry IV.
1400	Dies on 25 October; buried in Westminster Abbey.

The medieval worldview

The worldview that would have been shared by Chaucer and his European contemporaries was markedly different from that of today, and you need to gain an understanding of it if you are to make proper sense of Chaucer's writings. Much of the information that follows was automatic knowledge for any medieval person, and so explicit references to it rarely occur.

The physical universe

The universe had been created by God, and was finite, comprehensible and purposeful; it existed as a home for man. Every element could be explained and every element was interrelated, so that the place and functioning of one aspect of the universe could be understood within the operation of the whole structure.

The Ptolemaic system

The cosmological model accepted in the medieval period is known as the Ptolemaic system, being a refinement of the ideas propounded by the Egyptian astronomer Ptolemy in the second century AD. This model held sway for well over 1,000 years, and was only superseded by more modern models based on the Copernican system long after the end of the Middle Ages.

According to the Ptolemaic system, the universe consisted of nine concentric transparent crystal spheres, with the Earth at the centre. Each of the first seven spheres contained a planet: in order, the Moon, Mercury, Venus, the Sun, Mars, Jupiter and Saturn. The eighth sphere contained the fixed stars. The ninth sphere, the so-called *primum mobile* (prime mover), contained no planet of its own, but its motion imparted movement to all the other spheres. God, who existed outside the created universe, controlled the whole process. The universe was therefore thought to be a clock-like mechanism, and the sound made by the mechanism could be imagined, or in certain exceptional circumstances heard. This was the famed 'music of the spheres', a divine harmony that inspired many writers, artists and musicians.

Heaven was thought to be the area outside the created universe, which yields the idea of going 'up' to heaven. Heaven itself was unaffected by time, movement or change. Between the *primum mobile* and the Moon there was movement but no decay or change; everything was perfect and divine. Change was limited to events within the sphere of the Moon, and therefore on Earth. This explained weather systems, the atmosphere, and the whole idea of human life being sub-lunar — literally, below the Moon. Events on Earth were affected by the movement of all the spheres — hence belief in astrology — but events taking place on Earth itself only affected the universe as far as the Moon. The deaths of Julius Caesar and King Duncan in Shakespeare's plays, for example, therefore cause chaos in the natural world and in the skies. The Moon, being the closest planet to Earth, had the most influence on human affairs, which explains why 'lunatics' were thought of as being directly affected by the Moon. Hell, rather neatly, found its place at the centre of the Earth, simultaneously suggesting the idea of going 'down' to Hell and meaning that Hell was at the furthest possible remove from Heaven.

The Great Chain of Being

Parallel to the physical order in the structure of the universe was the logical order implied by the medieval belief in hierarchy. The system by which everything on Earth was believed to be organised is generally known as the Great Chain of Being. This categorised all of the items in the universe, with God at the top and inanimate matter at the bottom. The table below shows this hierarchy and the associated properties of each item.

Item	Properties
God	Reason, Movement, Life, Existence
Angels	Reason, Movement, Life, Existence
Man	Reason, Movement, Life, Existence
Animals	Movement, Life, Existence
Plants	Life, Existence
Inanimate matter	Existence

The hierarchy was governed by the universal principle that it is the duty of each creature to obey those higher up the hierarchy, and the responsibility of each creature to govern those below it. This gives rise to some important observations. First, it is the duty of all creatures to obey God. Equally, it is God's duty to govern his universe responsibly. Mankind was created 'in God's image', which means possessing the same attributes; it is the faculty of reason that sets humans apart from all other creatures on Earth. It is the duty of mankind to obey God and the messages conveyed by his angels; it is the responsibility of mankind to govern the Earth in accordance with God's wishes.

As with the universe itself, once this system is understood a large number of things make sense. The Fall of Man, the original sin when Adam and Eve disobeyed God (symbolically by eating an apple), entailed a fundamental violation of the Great Chain of Being, and it is no surprise that its consequences were therefore absolute. Genesis makes clear that their sin was to disrupt the hierarchy by believing themselves to be higher than they were — they fell prey to the devil's temptation that they would be 'as Gods, knowing good and evil'. Satan himself fell from heaven because of the same sin of pride, believing himself equal to God when his duty was to obey his natural superior. In the opposite direction, a medieval person would utterly condemn animal rights supporters for failure to understand the hierarchy. Over the last few centuries this sense of vertical hierarchy has been dismantled, so that many people no longer recognise a deity that is 'above' them, and equally refuse to claim superiority over creatures notionally 'below' them.

Hierarchies within the groups

Within each part of the hierarchy, further hierarchies existed, giving rise to the concept of 'degree' — one's exact positioning on the social scale. There was a hierarchy within the animals, which is why the lion is still often referred to as the 'king' of the beasts. Among human beings, several such hierarchies were visible. In secular society, the king was the sole ruler, followed by the nobility (themselves with several ranks) and then the rest; even among the peasants there were various gradings depending on their conditions of service or tenure. The parallel structure in the Church had the pope as the supreme authority, and a number of ranks from cardinal, archbishop and bishop down to parish priest and curate. In every case the same governing rule applied, which is why kings and popes could claim divine sanction for their rule and why regicide was viewed with such horror.

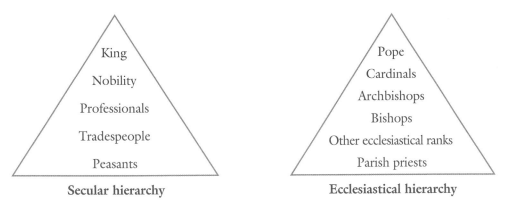

King
Nobility
Professionals
Tradespeople
Peasants

Secular hierarchy

Pope
Cardinals
Archbishops
Bishops
Other ecclesiastical ranks
Parish priests

Ecclesiastical hierarchy

The tension between the two hierarchies caused problems, most famously in the case of Thomas Becket. A friend and chancellor to Henry II, Becket was appointed by the king as Archbishop of Canterbury. Henry hoped that this would give him power over the Church, but Becket defied him and claimed that ecclesiastical authority was higher than secular authority. This led to Becket's assassination in 1170, and the start of the veneration of him as a saint that made Canterbury the leading pilgrimage site in England.

The final significant hierarchical distinction, and the one with the most far-reaching implications for Western society and history, was the claim that men were hierarchically superior to women, a doctrine founded on Genesis. This meant that men could and should rule over women, and women had to obey their husbands. Until recently, the standard Christian marriage service included the vow that the wife would obey the husband, but without the reciprocal promise of obedience from the man. Centuries of institutionalised inequality and anti-feminism were an automatic concomitant of such a belief, the repercussions of which are still felt today.

However, despite this notion of the relative status of men and women, the situation in reality was always more complex. Debate over the relative status, rights and responsibilities of men and women was as rife in Chaucer's time as it is today. There was a large corpus of antifeminist writing because most writers were male clerics, but it is clear that women were far from silent, as Chaucer reveals in his portrayal of the Wife of Bath. Much of *The Canterbury Tales* is concerned with this topic, with all kinds of relationships and attitudes being portrayed, and 'The Merchant's Tale' is a central part of the discussion.

Medieval society

The three estates model

Medieval society comprised three classes or estates: those who fought, those who prayed, and those who laboured to sustain the first two groups. In principle, this was the basis of feudal society, although the reality was never that simple.

The first estate was the clergy, a large group that maintained the fabric of society through the service of God and the regulation of human affairs. The second estate was the nobility, who were few in number, and were landowners and professional soldiers. The third estate was the vast bulk of ordinary people, who were subject to the laws of both the other groups. In a primarily agrarian society, this group comprised mainly peasants who laboured on the land to create the food and wealth by which society was sustained. A person was born into either the second or third estate, and might enter the first (the clergy) through vocation or for a variety of other reasons, including a desire for security or advancement. Otherwise, people were expected to remain in the rank to which God had allocated them at birth.

In addition to being members of one of the three estates, medieval women were also placed in three categories: virgin, wife and widow. They were thus sometimes thought of as a separate, fourth estate, inferior in consequence and importance to men.

In practice, the structure of medieval society was not as simplistic as the three estates model suggests, and by Chaucer's lifetime significant changes had taken place. From the start, there were inequalities in the third estate, which necessarily covered a vast range of occupations. With the passing of time people strove to better their conditions, and by the fourteenth century there were numerous distortions and anomalies within the system. The range of characters in *The Canterbury Tales* illustrates this. The only members of the nobility are the Knight and his son the Squire. The only true peasant is the Ploughman. There are several members of the clergy, but only three women. The remaining pilgrims all occupy a shifting middle ground; they are technically members of the third estate, but to equate the Man of Law — a wealthy, influential professional — with the Miller is clearly absurd. Although class distinctions continue to exist to this day, it is evident that the feudal division into classes had already lost much of its practical significance long before the end of the Middle Ages; *The Canterbury Tales* amply shows how there was a blurring of position, wealth and influence in this period.

Social change

The late fourteenth century was a time of great change, which makes *The Canterbury Tales* a valuable window onto an important period in English history.

The Black Death

The catalyst for change was the outbreak of the plague known as the Black Death. This swept through Europe and devastated England on several occasions in the fourteenth century, most radically in 1348–49, early in Chaucer's life. The exact figures are unknown, but estimates suggest that up to 40% of England's population died. The effects of this were colossal. Before the mid-fourteenth century, the population had been expanding, meaning that labour was plentiful and land use was intensive. Afterwards, labour became scarcer, but pressures on land decreased. Thousands of individual jobs and roles were lost. Inevitably, there was suddenly scope for enterprising people from all ranks of society to seek better conditions and better occupations.

The Peasants' Revolt

Social unrest was a likely outcome of social change, and it is not surprising that the uprising known as the Peasants' Revolt occurred in 1381. This rebellion was primarily triggered by increased taxation, and resulted in a march on the city of London and demands for the eradication of serfdom. The rebellion gained little of immediate consequence, but it offers an important insight into the way that society was changing at a rapid pace. At the time, Chaucer was living above Aldgate, one of the six city gates of London, so he must have had an intimate awareness of the events that took place.

Language

Further changes were probably hastened by the upheaval following the outbreaks of plague. It was during Chaucer's lifetime that English re-emerged as the official language of court and the law, supplanting the Norman French that William the Conqueror had imposed and paving the way for the dominance of what would become Modern English in the nation and beyond. This is reflected in Chaucer's choice of English for all his major works; by comparison, his friend John Gower wrote three major works, one in English, one in French and one in Latin.

The Church

Although it remained a paramount power both in politics and in society, the Church was also subject to upheaval at this time. In 1378, one of the years in which Chaucer visited Italy, the Great Schism took place. This was a rift in the Church which resulted in the election of two popes — an unimaginable situation if one considers the hierarchical significance of the pope as the appointed representative of God on Earth. The Italians had elected Urban VI as pope, but the French, supported by their king, Charles V, appointed Clement VII, who set up his throne in Avignon. Like the Peasants' Revolt, the Great Schism led to further questioning of the authority of established powers, and a greater willingness on the part of ordinary people to press their own claims for rights and privileges.

In England the effects of the upheaval in the Church were particularly felt in the work of John Wycliffe (1328–84), a reformer who attacked papal authority and denounced the Great Schism as 'Antichrist itself'. He argued that every man had the right to examine the Bible for himself, and sponsored the first translation of the Bible into English. He was a major figure in the latter part of the fourteenth century, and his work led to the heretical movement known as Lollardy. It is debatable whether or not Chaucer had Lollard sympathies; certainly his writing, in particular in *The Canterbury Tales*, attacks abuses within the Church in a way with which Wycliffe would have sympathised.

Medieval beliefs

The seven deadly sins

One of the most common and enduring aspects of medieval religious imagery is its focus on the seven deadly sins, references to which are still found in modern times, long after direct belief in such a system has faded. There is occasional variation in the list of sins, but this is the most common and is listed in the order in which they appear in 'The Parson's Tale':

English	Latin
Pride	Superbia
Envy	Invidia
Anger (wrath)	Ira
Sloth	Accidia
Avarice (greed)	Avaricia
Gluttony	Gula
Lust (lechery)	Luxuria

Pride is traditionally the chief of the sins because it incorporates all the others. It involves a false belief in one's own importance, and is the sin through which Lucifer fell and became Satan, and through which Adam and Eve fell, tempted to believe that they could be 'as gods'. Pride in one's opinion could lead to anger; pride in one's personal attributes could lead to lust.

Although occasional attempts have been made to demonstrate that the whole scheme of *The Canterbury Tales* is an exposition on the seven deadly sins, it is more fruitful to see them as an underlying part of medieval belief, and one which colours many of the portraits and the stories in *The Canterbury Tales*. Sometimes the symbolism is evident. The Wife of Bath's unrestrained sexual desire makes her guilty of lechery; the Monk is guilty of gluttony, because of his unrestrained desire for physical well-being; the Pardoner is avaricious. In other cases the particular sin of a character is more arguable; a harsh judgement of the Prioress would make her guilty of pride, whereas a more charitable one would accuse her of greed, the desire for worldly goods and status. The Merchant, who is 'Sowninge alwey th'encrees of his winning' ('The General Prologue', line 277), is a more obvious example of monetary avarice.

The four humours

Medieval science held that all matter was composed of four elements, each with its associated qualities which in turn gave rise to a human disposition known as the humour or temper. It was believed that different humours were predominant in individuals, dictating their temperament or 'complexioun', and that sickness arose when the balance of the humours was disturbed (an idea which survives in the modern phrase 'to be in a bad temper'). The qualities of each element, and the humour it was thought to cause, are given in the table below.

Element	Qualities	Humour	Personality
Earth	Cold and dry	Melancholy	Melancholic
Air	Hot and moist	Blood (sanguinity)	Sanguine (cheerful)
Fire	Hot and dry	Choler	Angry
Water	Cold and moist	Phlegm	Phlegmatic (unemotional)

Belief in the four humours was so ingrained in medieval society that it rarely receives specific treatment, but their consequences can be seen in a number of Chaucer's pilgrims in 'The General Prologue'. The Reeve is 'a sclendre colerik man' (line 589), his hot and dry nature having wasted his flesh away so that he is stick-like. The Franklin is also precisely identified: 'Of his complexioun he was sangwin' (line 335). The Wife of Bath has the ruddy complexion of a sanguine character too: 'Boold was hir face, and fair, and reed of hewe' (line 460). The Doctor's expertise (lines 421–23) is based on his understanding of the humours and his ability to diagnose and prescribe accordingly:

> He knew the cause of everich maladie,
>
> Were it of hoot, or coold, or moist, or drie,
>
> And where they engendred, and of what humour.

It is amusing that modern students of social behaviour often try to reduce personality to a schematic interpretation — sometimes even featuring four 'types' — that is little different from the medieval scheme.

Tradition and innovation

When reading Chaucer, it is essential to understand the different attitude to innovation that distinguishes the medieval period from the modern age. Nowadays, the emphasis in artistic creation is on originality; a writer or other artist who deliberately copies another, even with modifications, is guilty of plagiarism. Students are well aware of the dangers and the penalties incurred by including plagiarism in their essays.

In the Middle Ages, the reverse was true. Originality was viewed with extreme suspicion, while adherence to what was traditional, established and accepted was applauded. It is easier to understand this attitude by taking the medieval worldview into account. God had created the universe, the Bible was the word of God, the Earth had been created for mankind, and while men and women obeyed God all was well. Everything about the world was established and fixed; the purpose of art and learning was not to discover 'new' things, but to reveal the glory and majesty of God's creation. Science, in so far as it existed at all, had the same aim.

Authorities

This attitude towards innovation helps to explain the medieval insistence on authorities — 'auctoritees' in Middle English. One could not rely on one's own opinion or judgement; instead, it was necessary to justify points by reference to accepted and established authorities. Inevitably the Bible, as the revealed word of God, was the ultimate and prime authority, closely followed by the writings of the early Church fathers, including Augustine, Jerome, Tertullian and Gregory, all of whom feature heavily in Chaucer's works. However, almost any written authority that had survived from former times was likely to be taken up and quoted as occasion served, and it is common to find classical and Arabic sources, such as Ptolemy's *Almagest*, quoted as freely as Christian ones. *'The Merchant's Tale'* offers a clear insight into the variety and importance of authorities in medieval literature.

The writer's task was not therefore to invent new things, but to take traditional and established tales and retell them in fresh and entertaining ways. In the same way that modern folk singers are not expected to create new pieces but to offer a personal interpretation of traditional songs, so medieval artists were more highly valued when they were reusing material with which their audience would already have been familiar. Most of Chaucer's stories in *The Canterbury Tales* were well known; it is significant that where he does seem to have invented a story, as is the case in 'The Franklin's Tale', he claims that it is just a translation. The skill of the artist was in his personal interpretation and presentation of the material, and in this Chaucer excelled.

Chaucer and his contemporaries

Chaucer's place in the history of English literature

It was John Dryden in the seventeenth century who labelled Chaucer 'the father of English poetry'. The modern reader may share this belief, because Chaucer is the earliest writer who is still widely known. His language is the most accessible, and the most 'modern', of all the medieval authors, and his emphasis on apparently realistic characters and themes seems modern too. He championed the use of the **iambic pentameter** and the rhyming couplet in much of his work, and this **metre** became the staple of English verse for the next 500 years. He was well known both in his own lifetime and after; many writers, including Shakespeare, were influenced by him and used his work as a source. The term 'father of English poetry' thus contains considerable truth, but it is also a distortion and conceals facts of which the student of Chaucer needs to be aware.

Chaucer died 600 years ago in 1400. *Beowulf*, the earliest known masterpiece in English, was composed around AD 700. By that reckoning, Chaucer lived more than half way through the chronological history of English literature and represents part of a continuing tradition rather than being the inventor of a new one.

It is easy to explain both the error contained in the popular view of Chaucer and his pre-eminence. First, there is the matter of language. *Beowulf* was composed in Anglo-Saxon (also known as Old English), and even Chaucer's great contemporaries, such as William Langland and the anonymous author of *Sir Gawain and the Green Knight*, were writing in a style that dated back nearly 1,000 years. This was the so-called 'alliterative style', in which **alliteration** and a flexible rhythm were used to give lines shape and structure. In contrast, Chaucer wrote in a newfangled style influenced by French and Italian, using a set metre (mainly iambic pentameter in *The Canterbury Tales*) and rhyming couplets. His language was that used in London, and since London was the capital of England it was inevitable that Chaucer's language would be that which has come to predominate, and is therefore most familiar to subsequent generations. Moreover, until Chaucer's day there was very little 'literature' at all, in the sense of material that was ever written down. In a largely illiterate society, most culture was communicated orally, and written versions (including *Beowulf* itself) are fortuitous historical accidents. Most writing was done in Latin, the language of the educated (which essentially meant monks), and it is only from Chaucer's time onwards that there is a strong tradition of literature written in English.

Other works

Chaucer did not just write *The Canterbury Tales*. His other major work is *Troilus and Criseyde*, an 8,200-line poem written in a **metre** known as rhyme royal, a 7-line stanza in iambic pentameter, which he used in 'The Clerk's Tale' and 'The Prioress's Tale'. It is a tragic love story based on a supposed incident in the Trojan War; Chaucer borrowed the plot from Boccaccio, and it was later treated by Shakespeare and Dryden.

Chaucer also wrote a number of short verses, and several long poems of the type known as 'dream visions', in which the narrator falls asleep and dreams the events the poem relates. His interest in the status and role of women, a noticeable theme in *The Canterbury Tales*, is confirmed by *The Legend of Good Women*, which tells the stories of nine classical heroines, including Cleopatra and Thisbe.

Chaucer is famed for his wide reading and considerable education, which are illustrated by the fact that a number of his works are translations. He may have translated part of the *Roman de la Rose*, the vast thirteenth-century French poem that is a major source for and influence on Chaucer's own work; he specifically mentions it in 'The Merchant's Tale'. He translated from Latin *The Consolation of Philosophy* by Boethius, one of the best-known philosophical works in the Middle Ages (although it dates from the sixth century). Finally, he translated a scientific work, *A Treatise on the Astrolabe* (an instrument for measuring the position of the stars), which demonstrates the breadth of Chaucer's knowledge as well as confirming the interest in astrology visible throughout his work, for example in the description of the Doctor of Physic in 'The General Prologue', and the detail of Nicholas's learning in 'The Miller's Tale'.

Influences

A man as widely read as Chaucer would be familiar with all the great historical writers known in his time, together with many contemporaries. In addition, Chaucer's foreign travels on the king's business would have brought him into direct contact with the works of great European writers such as Boccaccio and Petrarch. Boccaccio's *Decameron* became a direct model for *The Canterbury Tales*. Chaucer was heavily influenced by biblical and religious writings, and by French and Italian writers of his own and previous centuries. It is worth thinking of him as a European rather than as a primarily English writer.

Numerous influences and sources, both general and specific, have been identified, and you should consult the edition of your text to appreciate the wealth of material on which Chaucer draws. The range of sources is particularly extensive in 'The Merchant's Tale' (see pp. 54–56).

Contemporaries

Chaucer is the best known of the fourteenth-century writers, but during this period there was a huge flowering of writing in English. This was probably because English was re-emerging as the official language of the country after three centuries of Norman French domination, and because greater education and literacy allowed the production of true literature, i.e work that was composed in writing rather than orally.

In Chaucer's own lifetime there were two other major English writers whose importance rivals that of Chaucer — William Langland and the Gawain-poet.

Langland

William Langland wrote the great poem *Piers Plowman*. He was obsessed with the work and wrote three versions of it, ranging from 2,500 to 7,300 lines, over a period of 30 or 40 years. It is written in the **alliterative** style, a completely different form of poetry from Chaucer's, and one which was a development of Anglo-Saxon verse. *Piers Plowman* is a vast allegorical work in which Piers begins as the figure of a humble ploughman (comparable to the Ploughman of 'The General Prologue') and ends up as an allegorical representation of Christ. It is deeply serious, complex, and unique.

The Gawain-poet

Meanwhile, perhaps in Cheshire, there was a poet to whom authorship of all four of the poems preserved in the *Pearl* manuscript is usually attributed. The poet's name is not known, but he is most commonly referred to as the Gawain-poet, after his most famous work, *Sir Gawain and the Green Knight*. Like *Piers Plowman*, this poem is written in an **alliterative** verse form, but its language is now so unfamiliar that it is usually read in a modernised version. It tells the story of a mysterious Green Knight who challenges King Arthur's court to a 'game' at Christmas. He invites someone to chop his head off, but when Gawain does so the Green Knight calmly collects his head and demands the right to return the blow in a year's time. The rest of the poem follows Gawain's dilemmas and tests as he seeks to keep his side of the bargain. The poem is a powerful, complex work that manages to be simultaneously humane and witty, profoundly moral and symbolic.

As well as these two writers there was John Gower, a personal friend of Chaucer's and a major influence on him, but whose works are no longer held in such esteem. He is best known for his *Confessio Amantis*.

The existence of these writers points to a vernacular tradition of enormous richness, variety and substance of which only a small portion has survived into the modern age. As well as Langland, the Gawain-poet and Gower, there was a wealth of material in all forms (poetry, drama and religious prose) that shows how Chaucer was part of a great age of literary output, rather than an isolated and unique genius.

Pilgrimage

The Canterbury Tales is based on two great defining structures: the story collection and the pilgrimage. The latter serves two purposes in the work. First, it is a **narrative** device, and second, it has a **thematic** function.

Narrative device

The role of pilgrimage in framing the narrative is simple but important. It gives Chaucer a basic plot — 30 pilgrims travel from London to Canterbury and back again — within which he can set out the multiple and varied narratives of his characters. It allows him to gather together a complete cross-section of the social hierarchy (excluding royalty, who would have travelled separately, and the very lowest serfs, who would not have been able to leave their work), in circumstances in which the characters can mingle on terms of near equality. This equality would have existed as regards their journey and experiences, but crucially there is equality of opportunity; every pilgrim gets the chance to tell a story, and every story receives the same attention, although what the pilgrims choose to do with their opportunities is another matter. The pilgrimage is also dynamic, so that circumstances on the journey can impinge on the storytelling framework, as happens when the pilgrims encounter a canon whose yeoman tells a tale of his own.

Thematic function

The second function of the pilgrimage in *The Canterbury Tales* is even more important. A pilgrimage has two aspects: it is a journey, but it is also a sacred journey. Both elements are crucial to an understanding of Chaucer's work.

Journeys

The image of the journey has always been central to human understanding. Life itself is conventionally seen as a journey from birth to death, and so any physical journey can be viewed as an image of life, with the travellers gaining experience as they progress. A pilgrimage is a special kind of physical journey, where the goal is a holy or sacred place. The parallel with the journey of life gains an extra significance, because the pilgrimage's sacred purpose is the equivalent of the soul's journey through life towards God. The best-known form of pilgrimage in modern times is the Muslim pilgrimage to Mecca, a journey that every devout Muslim is supposed to undertake at least once.

Holy sites and shrines

In the Middle Ages the pilgrimage was a common and popular activity and there were innumerable holy places to visit. The most holy site of all was Jerusalem, which the Wife of Bath visited three times, and Chaucer also mentions some of the other most famous ones, particularly Santiago de Compostela in Spain. In England, the shrine of Thomas Becket in Canterbury was the most popular destination following Becket's assassination in 1170, and it would remain so until it was destroyed by Henry VIII in the 1530s.

The importance of shrines lay in people's belief in the efficacy of saints and holy relics, as is evident from Chaucer's portrayal of the Pardoner. The Catholic Church taught that God could not be approached directly; it was therefore necessary to pray to those closest to him to intercede. Along with the Virgin Mary, with her unique position as the mother of Christ, the saints were thought to be endowed with special powers and influence. The relics of saints, particularly their bones, were held to have mystical, almost magical powers, and there were dozens of shrines associated with particular saints, each usually venerated for a specific quality.

Travel

Pilgrimage therefore held an important place in medieval life, but it was also a way to travel. In an insecure world, there was safety in numbers as well as the pleasure of company. Some of Chaucer's pilgrims, such as the Guildsmen, would be delighted to have a knight as part of the group, because he could offer practical as well as symbolic protection. A woman like the Wife of Bath would be pleased that the Guildsmen themselves were there, among whom she might look for her sixth husband; it would also have been difficult for her as a woman to travel alone.

It has been said that medieval pilgrimages were the equivalent of modern package holidays, and there is some value in the **analogy**, at least if it is seen as indicating the impulse to travel and the willingness of diverse people to band together for convenience and economies of scale. The comparison falls down, however, when the purpose of travel is considered. Modern holidaymakers largely seek pleasure, and few travel with an overtly spiritual purpose. The reverse was true in the Middle Ages; although a few of Chaucer's pilgrims might have purely social or secular motives for the journey, most would have a greater or lesser degree of devotion, and all would have been aware of the sacred significance of their journey, even if they sometimes chose to ignore it.

Symbolism

Every character, every tale, and every word of *The Canterbury Tales* is contained within the symbolic framework of the pilgrimage, whether the individual characters are aware of it or not. When the Parson tells his tale of sin and repentance the connection is obvious, but the symbolism of the pilgrimage is equally relevant when the Merchant is telling his tale of an ill-judged marriage, when the Miller and the Reeve are trading tales at each other's expense, or when the Pardoner tries to con his audience through the techniques that he has just exposed. Every one of these is measured against, and judged by, the sacred context in which their journey and their lives take place.

The route to Canterbury

The map shows the details of the pilgrimage in *The Canterbury Tales*, including the places mentioned by Chaucer in the text. The journey from London to Canterbury was nearly 60 miles long and would usually have taken several days in each direction.

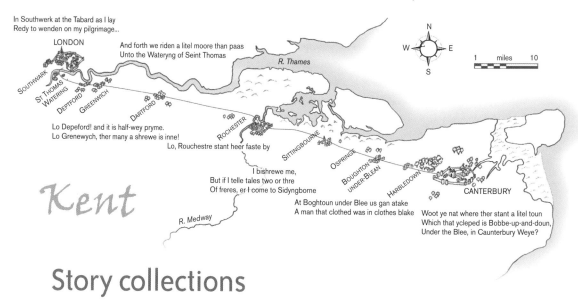

Story collections

In the Middle Ages, storytelling was a common form of communal entertainment. Literacy was scarce, and tales were told and retold, handed down from storyteller to storyteller through generations and centuries. Originally, almost all stories would have been in verse as this made them easier to remember, but as the Middle Ages progressed an increasing number were written in prose. Traditional stories might be gathered together by a scribe, and gradually individual storytellers emerged who adapted material to their own designs and added to it. Collections of stories therefore became common, some of which were mere agglomerations of tales, and others unified and written by a single author. A few of these collections are still well known, the most familiar example being *The Thousand and One Nights*.

Influences and contemporary examples

Chaucer would have been influenced by two particular works. The anonymous *Gesta Romanorum* was an amorphous and disparate group of tales gathered in various forms over a long period, but united by a single guiding principle. The tales, many of them traditional or legendary, were viewed as **allegories**, that is to say literal narratives that could be given a parallel spiritual interpretation. Each tale is followed by an explanation offering a Christian reading of the text. For example, the classical tale of Atalanta, the swift runner who is beaten by a competitor who throws golden apples to distract her from the race, is seen as an allegory of the human soul being tempted by the devil. It is worth considering how far *The Canterbury Tales* can similarly be seen as a diverse group of stories unified by an underlying Christian message. The *Gesta Romanorum* is also a vital reminder that medieval literature could be complex, and that medieval audiences expected multiple and concealed meanings in a work of art.

The second work, which may be considered as an immediate model for Chaucer, is the *Decameron* by Giovanni Boccaccio. Chaucer travelled to Italy and may have met Boccaccio; it is certainly true that he knew the Italian poet's work and was probably trying to create an equivalent masterpiece in English. The framework of the *Decameron* is similar to that of *The Canterbury Tales*, in that 10 narrators are given the task of telling 10 stories each over the course of 10 days, making a neat 100 stories in all. Chaucer's scheme has 30 narrators telling 4 stories each, making a more substantial total of 120 tales. The fact that this scheme came nowhere near completion, and that Chaucer probably reduced the plan to a single tale for each teller, does not reduce the significance of the comparison.

Chaucer's friend John Gower also produced a story collection, suggesting the popularity of such works in the fourteenth century. Gower's *Confessio Amantis* ('Confession of the Lover') is a moral work commenting on the **seven deadly sins**, the same theme as the sermon in 'The Parson's Tale'. Gower also used some of the same stories as Chaucer, notably the tale of Florent (also told by the Wife of Bath) and the tale of Constance ('The Man of Law's Tale').

The Canterbury Tales as a story collection

The difference between Chaucer's work and these other story collections is the dynamic link between the tellers and the tales. The *Gesta Romanorum* has no narrator at all; it is merely a collection of separate tales. Although there are ten separate narrators in the *Decameron*, there is no great significance in who tells which tale. In Chaucer's work, the match of tale and teller is frequently a crucial part of the overall meaning. The Knight, the most courtly figure on the pilgrimage, tells a suitably courtly tale. The Miller, the most vulgar of the pilgrims, tells the coarsest story. In the most sophisticated case, the Pardoner, who would be a profitable subject for modern psychoanalysis, introduces his tale by explaining the hypocritical success of his own sales techniques, and then proceeds to attempt to dupe his auditors in exactly the same way. As part of this he tells a devastatingly effective tale of greed and justice, which is integrally linked to both his personality and his practices.

The Canterbury Tales is remarkable because it contains examples of all the kinds of story popular in the medieval period — courtly tales, sermons, saints' lives, fabliaux, animal fables — and different verse forms, as well as two tales in prose. This makes *The Canterbury Tales* one of the most diverse of all story collections, and the **narrative** device of the pilgrimage plays an important part in giving this mix cohesion.

It can be difficult to appreciate the significance of Chaucer's overall scheme, both because of the unfinished nature of *The Canterbury Tales*, and because A-level students are usually restricted to studying a tale in isolation. It is strongly recommended that you acquaint yourself with *The Canterbury Tales* as a whole, perhaps by reading the complete work in Modern English.

Chaucer's audience and purpose

Audience

Chaucer was a courtly writer, composing his works for a courtly and sophisticated audience. In earlier eras, almost all culture would have been oral and communal, with storytellers and poets reciting their works to diverse groups of listeners. The only 'books' were manuscripts that were copied by hand onto parchment made from animal skins, and would have been rare and valuable. Almost all manuscripts were of religious texts, and it was not until the later Middle Ages that manuscripts of secular works like Chaucer's became available (more than 80 copies of *The Canterbury Tales* survive). By Chaucer's time, there were sufficient numbers of educated people and manuscript copies to enable private reading parties where one person, for example a lady of the court, would read stories to small groups of friends. An individual might even read stories alone, but that would necessitate the availability of a manuscript, and leisure to peruse it.

Despite these developments, the main mode of communication was still the public performance. It is helpful to think of Chaucer's original audience listening to *The Canterbury Tales* rather than reading them. No doubt Chaucer read his work to groups at court on frequent occasions, and his audience was mixed, with members of different social groups and classes present. In this sense, Chaucer's situation would have been similar to that of Shakespeare, who had to construct dramas that would appeal to the widest possible taste and intellect. *The Canterbury Tales* includes plenty of entertaining moments to elicit the most superficial of responses, yet also contains subtle and sophisticated elements.

Another development was that Chaucer was identified by name as an author and was popular in his own lifetime. Before this, almost all art was anonymous — the work of art mattered, not its creator.

Purpose

This consideration of Chaucer's audience leads to the vexed question of Chaucer's intentions in composing *The Canterbury Tales*, a subject to which there is no definitive answer.

Irony

Irony is the dominant tone throughout *The Canterbury Tales*, and this makes Chaucer's work elusive and his purpose difficult to define. Irony always depends on personal interpretation, but not all interpretations are equally justifiable or defensible, so be sure that yours are based on wide and careful reading.

An example will illustrate the need for thought. Consider line 99 in 'The Merchant's Tale':

A wyf is Goddes yifte verraily

An inattentive reader will simply accept this as a proverbial comment and pass on. A more considered response is to examine this line in its immediate context, which is the long early digression (lines 55–180) on the theme of marriage, and wonder who is speaking. If it is January, then he may genuinely believe the truth of what he is saying. If the passage is assumed to be by the narrator, then the Merchant is being cynical, as is evident from his own prologue. But the whole tale is Chaucer's work, and he may well wish to assert the truth of the remark, unless we believe him to be cynical too. The line also needs to be considered in the context of an overall reading of the tale, because May is hardly 'Goddes yifte' to January. Additionally, a feminist perspective might regard the remark as reflecting a typically male-orientated view of society. All these possibilities need to be weighed and considered, and a good A-level student will be able to handle the sophisticated response required.

Possible interpretations

Modern readers must make up their own minds as to what they are going to gain from studying Chaucer, and this is often a reflection of what they bring to their studies. You will probably find evidence for all the approaches suggested below, but it is up to you to decide what Chaucer has to offer, and how he is to be interpreted in the twenty-first century.

Entertainment

Chaucer's tales are entertaining, and some readers wish to look no further than that. John Carrington, in *Our Greatest Writers and their Major Works* (How To Books,

2003), says simply: 'Chaucer has no over-arching moral or philosophical intention', and that he 'is driven by a curiosity and sympathy for life that excludes the judgemental'.

Social comment

Many readers find some degree of comment on the behaviour and manners of medieval society. This could be anything from wry observation to serious **satire**, e.g. a satire on the three estates class system or a developed thesis on the nature of marriage.

Moral teaching

Chaucer himself, in the 'Retraction' included at the end of *The Canterbury Tales*, quotes from St Paul's comment in the New Testament that all literature contains a moral lesson.

Devotional literature

As a development of the previous point, readers may consider the Christian framework of *The Canterbury Tales* and the idea that it preaches specifically Christian doctrines. The vast majority of medieval literature is religious in this sense, e.g. the mystery plays, such as the Coventry and York cycles, are based on Bible stories. *The Canterbury Tales* finishes with 'The Parson's Tale', a sermon about the **seven deadly sins**, encouraging many to interpret them as having a Christian message about behaviour and morality.

Allegory

Medieval people were familiar with allegory, in which a surface narrative contains one or more further parallel layers of meaning. Such ideas were familiar from Christ's parables in the Bible, and the whole Bible was interpreted allegorically in the Middle Ages. It is possible to see Chaucer as an allegorist in whole or part; Robert P. Miller, writing in the *Companion to Chaucer Studies* (Oxford University Press, 1968), comments: 'Each pilgrim tells his tale from his own point of view, but this point of view is finally to be measured in the perspective afforded by the allegorical system.'

The framework of *The Canterbury Tales*

'The General Prologue' introduces *The Canterbury Tales* and establishes the framework that will underpin the diverse collection of tales that follow. It is worth considering the *Tales* as a whole to see what Chaucer was trying to achieve. It is well known that Chaucer left the work unfinished when he died in 1400, and it has traditionally been assumed that we have only a fragmentary part of what he would eventually have written.

The tales and their tellers

Chaucer's original plan, as revealed in 'The General Prologue', allowed for 30 pilgrims telling 4 tales each, making a total of 120 tales in all. However, only 24 tales exist, 4 of which are unfinished, and although as the *Tales* stand nearly every pilgrim tells a tale, they only tell 1 each.

It is clear that Chaucer drastically modified his original plan, although he never altered 'The General Prologue' to confirm this. There is an excellent reason for his changes. In Chaucer's hands, the tales and tellers are matched with great care, so that one illuminates the other. This is conspicuously true of characters such as the Wife of Bath and the Pardoner. To give these characters more than one tale would gain nothing, and would in fact weaken the effectiveness of the link between tale and teller. In this way Chaucer breaks out of the traditional mould of story collections, in which the character of the narrator is largely unimportant; *The Thousand and One Nights*, for example, has a single narrator for all of its diverse stories.

The significance of the connection between the pilgrims and their tales is emphasised by the only character to tell two tales: Chaucer himself. He starts off with the tale of 'Sir Thopas', but this is told so feebly that the Host (hardly the most astute of critics) interrupts him and tells him to stop. Chaucer thereby achieves the double effect of satirising the weak and formulaic narrative verse of his own time, and creating a joke against himself. His revenge is to let the pilgrim Chaucer follow up with 'a lytel thing in prose', the extended and deeply moral 'Tale of Melibee'. Given that the only other prose piece in *The Canterbury Tales* is 'The Parson's Tale', a meditation on penance, the author may well intend that the pilgrim Chaucer's tale be regarded as one of the most important pieces in the collection, although it is not at all to modern taste.

It is therefore likely that *The Canterbury Tales* is much nearer to completion than a consideration of Chaucer's original plan suggests. However, there are certain anomalies that Chaucer would have needed to address:

- The Yeoman, the Ploughman and the Five Guildsmen lack tales. The absence of 'The Ploughman's Tale' is a particular loss, given the iconic status of ploughmen, as established by Chaucer's contemporary William Langland in *Piers Plowman*.
- 'The Cook's Tale' and 'The Squire's Tale' are unfinished and simply break off part way through; the Knight interrupts the Monk, and the Host halts the doggerel tale of 'Sir Thopas'.
- There are occasional discrepancies in the assignation of tales to tellers; e.g. 'The Shipman's Tale' is clearly intended to have a female narrator.
- In several cases there is no significant connection between tale and teller, although this may be intentional.
- Some of the tales do not have links between them, and the final sequence of the tales is not established.

Taken as a whole, however, it is possible to discern a powerful and unified work that closely reflects Chaucer's final intentions.

The table below shows the order in which the pilgrims are introduced in 'The General Prologue' and the length of their tales.

Character	Lines in 'The General Prologue'	Number of lines	Tale	Number of lines in tale	Order in Robinson's edition
1 Knight	43–78	36	'The Knight's Tale'	2,250	1
2 Squire	79–100	22	'The Squire's Tale'	664	11 (unfinished)
3 Yeoman	101–17	17	–	–	–
4 Prioress	118–62	45	'The Prioress's Tale'	203	16
5 Second Nun	163–64	$1\frac{1}{2}$	'The Second Nun's Tale'	434	21
6–8 Three Priests	164	$\frac{1}{2}$	'The Nun's Priest's Tale'	626	20
9 Monk	165–207	43	'The Monk's Tale'	776	19 (unfinished)
10 Friar	208–69	62	'The Friar's Tale'	364	7
11 Merchant	270–84	15	'The Merchant's Tale'	1,174	10
12 Clerk	285–308	24	'The Clerk's Tale'	1,120	9
13 Man of Law	309–30	22	'The Man of Law's Tale'	1,028	5
14 Franklin	331–60	30	'The Franklin's Tale'	896	12
15–19 Five Guildsmen	361–78	18	–	–	–
20 Cook	379–87	9	'The Cook's Tale'	58	4 (unfinished)
21 Shipman	388–410	23	'The Shipman's Tale'	434	15
22 Doctor of Physic	411–44	34	'The Physician's Tale'	286	13
23 Wife of Bath	445–76	32	'The Wife of Bath's Tale'	408	6
24 Parson	477–528	52	'The Parson's Tale'	1.005 (prose)	24
25 Ploughman	529–41	13	–	–	–
26 Miller	542–66	25	'The Miller's Tale'	668	2
27 Manciple	567–86	20	'The Manciple's Tale'	258	23
28 Reeve	587–622	36	'The Reeve's Tale'	403	3
29 Summoner	623–68	46	'The Summoner's Tale'	586	8
30 Pardoner	669–714	46	'The Pardoner's Tale'	506	14
31 Chaucer	–	–	'Sir Thopas'	207	17 (unfinished)
			'The Tale of Melibee'	922 (prose)	18
32 Canon	–	–	–	–	–
33 Canon's Yeoman	–	–	'The Canon's Yeoman's Tale'	762	22

The multiple narrator in *The Canterbury Tales*

In a conventional novel, the action is mediated to the reader by a narrator:

Narrator
⬇
Audience

In *The Canterbury Tales*, Chaucer introduces further **narrative** levels that offer the opportunity for much greater subtlety. First, Chaucer the author introduces himself as a character or persona within the text, so that the situation is as follows:

Chaucer the author
⬇
Chaucer the pilgrim
⬇
Audience

This means that when you come across a remark in 'The General Prologue' like 'And I seyde his opinion was good', it is ostensibly made by Chaucer the pilgrim. The reader must decide how far it may also be Chaucer the author's view.

When it comes to the tales themselves, a further layer of complexity is added because each tale is told by one of the pilgrims and reported by Chaucer the pilgrim. The narrative reaches its audience at three removes from its author:

Chaucer the author
⬇
Chaucer the pilgrim
⬇
Pilgrim narrator
⬇
Audience

Finally, when a character within one of the tales speaks a fifth narrative layer is added:

Chaucer the author
⬇
Chaucer the pilgrim
⬇
Pilgrim narrator
⬇
Character
⬇
Audience

The attentive reader must decide how far each of the narrating figures is in accord with what is being said. For example, January, the old husband in 'The Merchant's Tale' (lines 52–53), says:

For wedlok is so esy and so clene,
That in this world it is a paradis.

The reader needs to consider how far January is being sincere (he is, but he's deluded about his own state), how far the Merchant agrees with him (he doesn't), what Chaucer the pilgrim's view would be (amused indulgence), and finally what Chaucer the author intends to convey about the sacrament of marriage. This last question is simultaneously the most important and, because of all the intervening narrative layers, the most difficult to decide, and it is why critical debate about Chaucer is unending.

Chaucer the pilgrim as narrator

The subtlety in Chaucer's craft arises from the device of the pilgrim narrator. This persona is portrayed as a sociable but rather diffident character. When the time comes for him to tell his own tale the Host thinks he looks 'elvyssh' (otherworldly) and shy: 'For evere upon the ground I se thee stare' ('Prologue to Sir Thopas', line 697). Chaucer the pilgrim begins to tell a poor story ('Sir Thopas'), but once interrupted by the Host he launches into a long, moral, prose narrative ('The Tale of Melibee'), which shows his erudition and seriousness. In 'The General Prologue', Chaucer the pilgrim frequently appears to be naive, most famously when he agrees with the Monk's low opinion of his own vows ('And I seyde his opinion was good', line 183). Often this encourages the other pilgrims to make further indiscreet confessions about their behaviour, such as the Monk revealing his obsession with hunting and riding. When Chaucer the pilgrim does wish to comment directly on a character, he can do so, as in the case of the Summoner: 'But wel I woot he lied right in dede' (line 661).

Chaucer's verse

The **metre** that Chaucer adopted for most of *The Canterbury Tales* became the standard one used in English poetry for the next 500 years, and in this sense at least he should be familiar to the modern reader. He writes in **iambic pentameter**, the metre used by Shakespeare, Milton, Keats and all of the great poets prior to the twentieth century. The lines are arranged into pairs called **heroic couplets**.

'Iambic' refers to the rhythm of the verse: a repeated pattern of two syllables, with the first syllable being unstressed and the second syllable being stressed, as in words like 'remind' and 'believe'. An iamb is one of these two-syllable, unstressed/stressed patterns. Each pair of syllables is called a foot. 'Pentameter' (literally five measures or 'feet') means that five feet are joined together to make a ten-syllable (decasyllabic) regular line: da dum da dum da dum da dum da dum. The conventional mark for a stressed syllable is /, and the mark for an unstressed syllable is ~. A couplet of iambic pentameter therefore goes like this:

~   / ~/ ~ / ~ / ~ /
And certeinly, as sooth as God is king,

~ / ~ /~ /~ / ~ /
To take a wif it is a glorious thing,...   ('The Merchant's Tale', lines 55–56)

The reason that this became the staple metre of English poetry is because iambic rhythm is closest to natural speech — whenever you speak a sentence, it contains more iambs than any other rhythm.

Chaucer shows astonishing assurance and versatility in handling the iambic form. He can use it for stately formal descriptions:

> Al ful of joye and blisse is the paleys,
> And ful of instrumentz and of vitaille,
> The mooste deyntevous of al Itaille: (ibid., lines 500–02)

He can use it for fast-paced action:

> And sodeynly anon this Damyan
> Gan pullen up the smok, and in he throng.   (ibid., lines 1140–41)

He uses it for rhetorical declamation by the narrator:

> O perilous fyr, that in the bedstraw bredeth;
> O famulier foo, that in his service bedeth;   (ibid., lines 571–72)

But most frequently and most effectively he uses it to represent speech:

> Now wol I speke of woful Damyan,
> That langwissheth for love, as ye shul heere;   (ibid., lines 654–55)

> 'Out, help; allas, harrow!' he gan to crye,
> 'O stronge lady stoore, what dostow?'   (ibid., lines 1154–55)

In his earlier work, Chaucer frequently used an octosyllabic (eight-syllable) line, which was common at the time; the iambic pentameter marks his maturity as a poet.

Chaucer's language

There is no doubt that the Middle English of *The Canterbury Tales* comes between the modern reader and an easy appreciation of the work. However, after a little practice most of the difficulties presented by the language drop away. Note that the vocabulary can present problems, because some words look familiar or obvious, and aren't. For example, the word 'wood' can mean wood but, in a different context, means mad, as in the description of Damyan in 'The Merchant's Tale' (line 563). The solution is to keep a careful eye on the notes and glossary of your edition.

Reading aloud

The easiest way to start to understand Chaucer's language is to read it aloud, or to listen to it being read. Chaucer intended his verse to be spoken, and it makes more sense when it is. Remember the following:

- Most letters are pronounced, so that 'knight' sounds like 'cnicht' and 'mighte' like 'micht'.
- The final 'e' on words like 'fooles' ('fool-es') is normally pronounced, unless it is followed by another vowel.
- Some vowels have different sound values, but don't worry about this initially.
- Words imported from French would still sound French, so 'dotage' would be 'dotarge' and 'mariage' would be 'mar-ee-arge'.

With these few simple adjustments, aim to read the verse as if it were ordinary conversation. Try to ignore the rhythm and rhyme — they'll take care of themselves. Your edition should have further detail on aspects of pronunciation, but the primary objective is to get a sense of the flow of the language.

Modernisations

Another good way of gaining confidence in reading the language is to create a Modern English version of each line. This can be done aloud in class, or you can jot down a literal version as you go along, for example:

> Whilom ther was dwellinge in Lumbardye
> *Once there was living in Lombardy*
> A worthy knight, that born was of Pavie,
> *A noble knight, who was born in Pavia*

It isn't long before Chaucer's English becomes almost as straightforward as Shakespeare's. You never quite lose your caution in looking at it (as you shouldn't with Shakespeare), but you do become more comfortable working with it.

It may be a good idea to obtain a modern version of 'The Merchant's Prologue and Tale', and even of the whole of *The Canterbury Tales*. This will allow you to check your own rendering of each line, so that you are confident that you have the correct basic meaning.

The Merchant in 'The General Prologue'

This is how the Merchant is introduced in 'The General Prologue' (lines 272–86). The modernised English version (in italics) is entirely literal, and is given to help clarify the meaning of the passage.

> A MARCHANT was ther with a forked berd,
> *There was a merchant with a forked beard*
> In mottelee, and hye on horse he sat;
> *Dressed in motley, who sat high on his horse;*
> Upon his heed a Flaundrissh bever hat,
> *With a Flemish beaver-skin hat on his head*
> 275 His bootes clasped faire and fetisly.
> *And boots with neat and attractive bindings.*
> His resons he spak ful solempnely,
> *He spoke with great dignity,*
> Sowninge alwey th'encrees of his winning.
> *Always harping on his profits.*
> He wolde the see were kept for any thing
> *He wanted the sea kept clear (of pirates) at all costs*
> Bitwixe Middelburgh and Orewelle.
> *Between Middelburg (in Holland) and Orwell (in Essex).*
> 280 Wel koude he in eschaunge sheeldes selle.
> *He was skilled at foreign exchange dealings.*
> This worthy man ful wel his wit bisette:
> *This worthy man used his wits well —*
> Ther wiste no wight that he was in dette,
> *Nobody knew that he was in debt,*
> So estatly was he of his governaunce
> *He was so dignified in his behaviour*
> With his bargaines and with his chevissaunce.
> *With his bargaining and money dealing.*
> 285 For sothe he was a worthy man with alle,
> *Indeed he was altogether a worthy man,*
> But, sooth to seyn, I noot how men him calle.
> *But, to tell the truth, I don't know his name.*

The portrait of the Merchant is one of the subtlest in 'The General Prologue' and the subject of a wide range of responses from critics and readers. The most common view is that the Merchant is a character who attempts to portray himself in a favourable light, but the reality undermines this pretension. As is often the case, Chaucer makes no direct criticism, and the reader should examine each detail of his description to make a judgement, bearing in mind Chaucer's characteristic use of irony.

Deceptive appearances

The Merchant is well dressed, with his 'Flaundrissh bever hat' and his 'bootes clasped faire and fetisly' (lines 274–75), and fashionable with his 'forked berd' and 'mottelee' (lines 272–73). He has all the appearance of a successful merchant — and this is the key to the portrait. His appearance is called into question through a number of ambiguous remarks, most notably in the lines following the initial description. Line 276, 'His resons he spak ful solempnely', seems promising: 'solempnely' (meaning 'with dignity' or 'impressively') suggests a serious and purposeful man, but it is undercut by the next line, 'Sowninge alwey th'encrees of his winning'. 'Sowninge' means to dwell on or to proclaim, and to keep boasting about one's profits is an unattractive quality. The 'solempne' begins to gain overtones of pomposity or of being boringly repetitive, which is cemented shortly afterwards by line 282, 'Ther wiste no wight that he was in dette'. Although it is possible that nobody knew he was in debt because he wasn't, the line clearly implies that he was, and line 277 becomes damning — he proclaims 'th'encrees of his winning' to hide the fact that he is making losses.

There is no need to enter the recent critical debate of whether the Merchant's foreign exchange dealings were legal or not. The clear tenor of the portrait is that the Merchant is self-seeking and self-aggrandising; the fact that he wants the seas kept clear of pirates is not from any altruistic motives about national security, but merely because they threaten his own trade. In this context his 'estatly…gover-naunce' (line 283) looks empty, and the observation that 'hye on horse he sat' (line 273) hints at a man who tries to look more impressive than he is.

The ending

As so often occurs in 'The General Prologue', the ending of the portrait needs particular consideration. The final couplet contains two **ironies**. Line 285, 'he was a worthy man with alle', is superficial praise entirely subverted by the ironic comments that precede it. This is followed by the apparently casual, 'But, sooth to seyn, I noot how men him calle'. Chaucer does not name many of the pilgrims, but the Merchant is the only one for whom he specifically proclaims that he doesn't know his name. The pretentious Merchant, who so wants to be admired, receives the rebuff of being left a nameless nonentity.

There is of course no compulsion to accept this reading of the Merchant, and certainly if lines are read literally rather than ironically much of the criticism falls away; what remains is a conventional portrait of a member of the emergent middle class, interesting because it captures a moment in social history when the established

order of wealth and privilege was undergoing significant changes. However, the portrait should be studied in relation to the more developed picture of the character that emerges from the tale he tells.

The 'marriage group' of tales

The term 'marriage group' was coined by the critic G. L. Kittredge in his seminal essay 'Chaucer's discussion of marriage', published in *Modern Philology Volume IX* (1911–12). Although some of his ideas now seem outdated, this remains an important discussion of Chaucer's work and intentions. You can find the entire text of this essay on the internet at www.courses.fas.harvard.edu/~chaucer/canttales/franklin/marriage.html.

Kittredge claimed that there is a sequence of stories in *The Canterbury Tales* that forms a closely-knit exploration of marriage. The sequence starts with 'The Wife of Bath's Prologue and Tale' and, after a digression between the Friar and the Summoner, is continued in the tales of the Clerk, Merchant, Squire and Franklin. The brief summary of these tales that follows helps to place 'The Merchant's Tale' in its proper context.

'The Wife of Bath's Prologue and Tale'

The Wife's prologue, which at 800 lines is longer than many of the other pilgrims' tales, tells of her personal experience of marriage. She has had five husbands, and has treated them mercilessly, until the fifth fights back and reads antifeminist writings to her, although he is eventually forced to concede 'maistrie' (mastery) to her. This prologue is an important setting for the ensuing debate about 'good' and 'bad' marriages.

The Wife of Bath then tells a tale of a knight who rapes a maiden. Condemned to death, he is given a year to find the answer to the question: 'What do women most desire?' He meets a hideous old hag who promises to give him the answer if he will do anything she asks. He is forced to agree, and having saved his life with the answer that women most desire dominance over their husbands, she demands that he marries her. On their wedding night he is revolted by her appearance, but she reproaches him for his lack of knightly courtesy. She poses him a further challenge by offering to be ugly but faithful, or beautiful but potentially adulterous. Unable to choose, he grants her 'maistrie' over him too, and is rewarded with her magical transformation into a beautiful and faithful young woman.

'The Friar's Tale'

The Friar and the Summoner, who tell their tales next, are not part of the 'marriage group', but are included here to show the sequencing of this part of *The Canterbury*

Tales. Like the Miller and the Reeve, they are mutually antagonistic, and tell tales at each other's expense.

The Friar's tale is about a summoner who meets a devil in the guise of a yeoman. They agree to work as partners. When they come across a carter who is cursing his horses and wishes the devil would take them, the summoner invites the devil to take the carter at his word; however, the devil is unable to snatch the horses because what the carter says is not what he truly wants. The summoner goes into a widow's house to demand money, and when she refuses he threatens to take her new pan instead. She wishes him and the pan to the devil; the devil asks her to confirm her wish, and when she does so he carries the summoner off to Hell.

'The Summoner's Tale'

The Summoner, infuriated by the Friar, tells the story of a greedy friar who visits a bedridden man. The man protests that all his gifts to the friars have not aided his recovery, but the friar still asks him for a further donation. The man invites him to put his hand in his bed to receive a rich gift, but when the friar does so the 'gift' is a huge fart. The friar protests about this treatment to the lord of the village but gains little sympathy, and a young squire solves the problem of how the gift can be divided equally among the friars.

'The Clerk's Tale'

An Italian marquis, Walter, marries a beautiful young woman, Griselda, who promises that she will never willingly disobey him. After the birth of their daughter, Walter is seized with an urge to test Griselda's faithfulness; he has the baby taken away, and says it is going to be murdered. On the birth of a son, he does the same thing. Griselda patiently accepts all this, but Walter is not satisfied. He pretends to have their marriage annulled, says he wants a younger wife, and insists that Griselda attends the wedding. Griselda remains patient, and is rewarded with the return of her two children and the eternal faithfulness of Walter.

'The Merchant's Tale'

January, a 60-year-old knight and womaniser from Lombardy in Italy, decides to marry. He sends for his friends to advise him, and although he sounds pious he wants to marry quickly and to have a young wife. Ignoring what is said to him, he pursues his own desires, and finds a pretty young woman called May. They marry, and he hurries everyone away from the marriage feast so that he can enjoy his wedding night.

Meanwhile his young squire, Damyan, is himself sick with love for May. When January sends May to comfort him, the two exchange letters and seek an opportunity to meet. Their chance arrives when January suddenly becomes blind. Despite his jealousy and watchfulness, the lovers contrive a plot to meet in the garden where January spends time with May.

May prompts January to take her to the garden one day. She climbs a tree, where Damyan is already hidden, and they have sex. January's sight is magically restored, but May persuades him that this is a direct result of her actions, and that he has a mistaken view of what has taken place. January accepts this and is overjoyed with his restored sight and with her.

'The Squire's Tale'

This is one of the unfinished stories in *The Canterbury Tales*, and is a romance. King Cambyuskan has a beautiful daughter, Candace. At a feast a strange knight appears, bearing magical gifts: a flying horse, a ring that enables the wearer to understand birds' speech, and a magical sword. Candace wears the ring and hears a falcon complaining because she has been deserted by her lover. Candace takes the falcon back to the palace, but after an indication of some of what is to follow, the tale breaks off.

'The Franklin's Tale'

For Kittredge, this final tale in the group seems to offer the perfect solution to the marriage problem. A knight in Brittany, Arveragus, marries a lady, Dorigen, and they make an agreement that although Arveragus will maintain the illusion of male authority, in reality they will be equal partners. While he is away in England, Dorigen fears for his safe return because of the rocks on the coast. A young squire, Aurelius, promises to remove the rocks if she will love him, and in an unguarded moment she promises to do so. Aurelius pays a magician to make the rocks seemingly disappear, and claims Dorigen's love. Arveragus returns and says that she must keep her promise, but Aurelius, seeing her distress, frees her from her word. The magician in turn relinquishes his payment, and the Franklin celebrates the generosity of all the parties involved.

Making sense of the story

January's justification for marrying

January is old, and claims that he wishes to know 'thilke blisful lyf' (line 47) that marriage brings; he refers to it as a 'paradis' (line 53), and thinks of it as a happy state (line 183). He tells his friends that he has led a sinful life, and wants to amend this by marrying before he dies (lines 188–92). He also desires heirs so that his estates will not pass to strangers (lines 225–28). His wish for a young wife is excused by the claim that an old wife would not satisfy him, and he would then be adulterous (lines 220–24). However, it is obvious from the start that the truth is more complex than this, and these justifications are largely excuses.

The digression in lines 55–180

These lines are devoted to the subject of marriage. They therefore relate specifically to this tale, and act as a commentary on January's situation and motives, and also on the Merchant's purpose in telling the tale. They are a significant contribution to the wider debate on marriage that Chaucer creates in *The Canterbury Tales*.

It is not clear who is speaking: medieval manuscripts do not use quotation marks. This uncertainty is a useful reminder that there are potentially four voices simultaneously at work here — January, the Merchant, Chaucer the pilgrim and Chaucer the author — each with a separate purpose. This can be a fruitful area for examining the complexity of medieval literature.

The advice of Placebo and Justinus

Placebo (Latin for 'I will please') is a sycophant who merely tells people what they wish to hear (lines 266–88), and therefore advises January to do whatever he wants. Despite his name, Justinus does not offer impartial advice. He is cynical and bitter, being unhappily married himself (lines 332–33), and acts as the mouthpiece of the Merchant: he warns January that it is difficult even for a young man to keep his wife to himself (lines 347–49).

Unsurprisingly, January reacts angrily to Justinus's cynicism and positively to Placebo, and decides to continue with what he was intending to do anyway.

January's attitude to May

'Love is blind' (line 386). January imagines May's physical beauty (lines 388–90) and sober character (lines 391–92), and talks of the 'parfit felicitee' (line 430) that the marriage will bring, 'withouten wo and stryf' (line 434). Note the warning given by Justinus at this point, 'Paraunter she may be youre purgatorie' (line 458).

The actual marriage is described in terms of a legal contract (lines 485–86), which undermines the romantic element. At their marriage feast, January is consumed with lust to the exclusion of all else (lines 538–52).

The wedding night

This is one of the comic highlights of the tale. January has to seek the help of drugs to increase his 'corage' (lines 595–600) and romantic love (lines 609–11) is sharply contrasted with the reality of the old man's body (lines 612–14, 637). The distinction between work (lines 620–22) and play (lines 623, 629) leads to the humiliating word 'laboureth' (line 630) to describe January's attempts at lovemaking. His speech (lines 616–19) and singing (lines 633–34) are revolting and ridiculous. The whole episode is capped by May's attitude (lines 639–42), which Chaucer carefully leaves until the very end.

Damyan

Damyan is presented in conventional terms as a lovelorn young man (lines 562–67) who falls sick because of his unrequited passion. He is left until this point in the story for two reasons:

- The narrative up to this point has focused on establishing the unsuitable marriage of January and May.
- Only when January and May are married does the chance for adultery arise. Damyan is introduced at the first possible point, dramatically speaking.

Damyan and May

Their love affair develops through letters, as they have no chance to speak directly to each other. When Damyan is sick in bed (because of his love for May), January ironically sends May herself to comfort Damyan. This gives Damyan the chance to give her the letter that he has written. She reads the letter and destroys it, and then writes him a letter in return. He instantly recovers from his sickness (lines 797–98), but they are unable to communicate further.

The significance of the garden (lines 817ff.)

Although the garden seems a natural place, in literature gardens almost always have important symbolic functions, and this is certainly true in this case:

- It is symbolic of the Garden of Eden, an earthly paradise (line 120). It too contains a dangerous fruit tree that represents temptation.
- It is entirely private, almost like a chastity belt for May — whoever possesses the key can possess her.

January's blindness

Chaucer offers no naturalistic explanation for January's blindness at all. His affliction is ascribed to Fortune or chance (lines 845–56). This may be to emphasise the symbolic significance of the situation; in symbolic terms, January is already blind (cf. line 386), and so the physical event is merely an outward manifestation of his inward state.

The development of the affair between Damyan and May

May seizes the opportunity of January's blindness to make a wax impression of the key to the garden (line 905), from which Damyan creates a duplicate that allows him access. This is achieved despite the fact that January never lets go of May.

At some point May writes another letter to Damyan explaining what is to happen in the garden, although this is not referred to until later (lines 1000–04).

The digression in lines 1007–107

The digression concerning the visit of Pluto and Proserpine to the garden is prefigured in lines 826–29. It has three purposes:

- It creates dramatic suspense, delaying the **denouement** of the tale for 100 lines.
- It is **thematic**, because their discussion is on the topic of marriage. The nature of their own marriage is an issue, as Pluto originally abducted Proserpine by force in one of the most famous classical **myths**. Their dispute is only resolved when Pluto gives in (line 1100), whereupon Proserpine agrees to be at peace with him again (line 1107) — a situation suggesting the henpecked and submissive husband, and highly reminiscent of the resolution of 'The Wife of Bath's Tale'.
- It provides the supernatural mechanism for the comic denouement of the tale, in which January magically regains his sight and yet May is able to deceive him against the evidence of his own eyes.

The climax of the tale

January and May arrive at the foot of the pear tree where Damyan is hiding. May pretends that she is pregnant (line 1123), and therefore has a craving for fruit. She asks January to circle the tree with his arms because he distrusts her, while she climbs it; she even stands on his back to help her up into it.

Once there, Damyan and May have sex without any preliminaries or sentiment (lines 1140–41). Pluto immediately restores January's sight, and he is horrified by what he sees. May instantly replies that she has in fact been the agent for restoring his sight by 'struggling' with a man in a tree (line 1162). January protests that this is not how it appears, but she persuades him that his restored sight is as yet faulty, and that he is mistaken (line 1198).

The outcome is that January is delighted to be able to see again, and takes her home as lovingly as ever — blind once again, despite having his physical sight restored. No mention is made of Damyan or of further events.

Characters

January

January is by far the most complex character in 'The Merchant's Tale'. He is also the most developed, having nearly 200 lines of dialogue. His stated motives are never quite sufficient to explain his actions, and his attitude to May changes as the story progresses. It is easy to develop a modern explanation for his personality in terms of obsession and self-delusion, but as you analyse the character bear in mind both that there were no psychological theories in the Middle Ages, and that the tale is frequently unrealistic in its events.

January is a knight and therefore a nobleman, a member of the highest rank of society. He is obviously rich and can therefore more or less please himself, as he does in his marriage to May. It is worth comparing him to the Knight in 'The

General Prologue', whose worthiness and dedication to the ideals of knighthood are in strong contrast to January.

One of Chaucer's great achievements is the way in which January is revealed to be self-deceiving. From the line 'Were it for hoolinesse or for dotage' (line 41), Chaucer builds a complex web in which there appears to be a genuine thread of sanctimonious desire in January to set his account straight before he dies (lines 188–92), and a natural wish to produce a legitimate heir (lines 220–28). This is rapidly overlaid, however, by a growing obsession with the idea of a young wife in general ('Heigh fantasye', line 365) and then with May in particular (lines 538–39). Despite, or perhaps because of, his earlier womanising (lines 37–38), he seems obsessed in his old age with the idea of possessing a young woman entirely as his own, so that he may do anything he likes with her (lines 623–28).

The portrait of January may seem unnervingly realistic in a psychological sense. This does not mean that Chaucer was a psychologist, nor even that January is intended as a realistic portrayal of a state of mind. It just means that Chaucer understood people and was adept at presenting them in his poetry. You may wish to pursue a 'psychological' interpretation of this and other Chaucerian characters, as is often done with *Hamlet*, but you need to bear in mind that January's function is primarily symbolic.

If nothing else, the name 'January' should be kept firmly in mind. He is winter to May's spring, and it is the unsuitability of their union that is at the heart of the Merchant's purpose in telling the tale. The Roman god Janus was two-faced (looking back to the old year and forward to the new), and January has divided motives.

A good starting point for discussing these different aspects of medieval characterisation is to examine lines 538–52. In one sense they reveal an extremely modern, psychological and interior depiction of the height of sexual desire; in another, they can be seen as a typically medieval illustration of lust, one of the **seven deadly sins**.

May

For much of the tale, May is merely the embodiment of the pretty young wife who is subject to a jealous old husband — a traditional role. She is not named until line 481 of the tale, her attitude to the situation is not considered until more than halfway through the story (line 642), and her voice is not heard until line 976 (although her thoughts are reported in line 770).

It is difficult for the reader to sympathise much with May — as no doubt the Merchant intended. His tale is about the dangers of marriage, so he would hardly wish to create an interesting heroine at the centre of it. Indeed, there is little in the tale to make May seem individual. She is conventionally pretty, and conventionally deceives her old husband by scheming with a young lover. Such individuality as there is might be found in her speech, but she is mute until late on in the tale and only has 65 lines of dialogue, against nearly 200 for January. When she does speak she is assertive and direct, but there is nothing here that is different from Alison in 'The Miller's Tale', or the Wife of Bath.

You may of course wish to argue otherwise, particularly if you are studying the tale in isolation rather than in comparison to the whole of *The Canterbury Tale*, or if you wish to emphasise the feminist aspects of the tale. A feminist reading would view May as an active protagonist who wants to direct the course of her own life and who is not willing to submit to her husband's demands. However, such an interpretation will need to account for the very end of the tale, when January leads her back home (line 1203).

At the same time, you may well be able to identify with May and recognise her responses. Her view of January's attempts at lovemaking (line 642) is inevitable, given the revolting description of his physical appearance, and so is the fact that she falls instantly in love with Damyan when she receives his letter; he is an attractive and virile young man, in contrast to her husband. The description of their intercourse at the end of the tale (lines 1140–41) is deliberately coarse, in order to divest the scene of any romantic aspect and to emphasise merely the foolishness of January.

Damyan

Damyan is a typical courtly lover. He falls in love with May without any opportunity of knowing her closely; he instantly falls sick and has to retire to his bed, and instantly recovers when he discovers that his love is returned.

He is a squire, a member of the nobility studying to become a knight. He is serving his apprenticeship in January's household, although there does not seem to be any kinship between them. As with January, it is worth comparing Damyan with his counterpart in 'The General Prologue', the Squire; in this case there seem to be several similarities between them. They both fulfil a squire's duties, including carving at table, they are both young lovers, and the Squire is even described as being 'as fressh as is the month of May' ('The General Prologue', line 92).

Damyan is an entirely conventional representation both of the courtly lover and of the young man who serves as the agent for cuckolding a foolish old husband. He only speaks two lines (lines 730–31), and is notably silent in the last 100 lines of the tale. He does not participate in the **dialogue** between May and January after the latter regains his sight, and is absent from the last few lines when they return home.

He is an appropriate lover for May in that he performs the single function of being a virile young man, but apart from this Chaucer takes no interest in him. His intercourse with May is solely physical, without affection or sentiment, and this conveniently leaves the reader without sympathy or concern for him as a character. The reader's attention is entirely given to January and May.

Placebo and Justinus

These are symbolic characters. Placebo's name literally means 'I will please' in Latin (compare the modern idea of a placebo in medicine, which is a drug that makes the patient better although it has no medicinal content), while Justinus's name suggests that he will be fair-minded and independent — the voice of justice.

Placebo's name suits him absolutely. He confesses that he never contradicts the opinion of people he is talking to, and therefore sycophantically praises January's wisdom and understanding, and encourages him to do whatever he chooses. In discussing Chaucer's characterisation it is worth noting that Placebo's function is entirely symbolic, yet Chaucer manages to give the illusion of a realistic individual through the dialogue, e.g. lines 279–92.

Justinus is a more complex case. At first he appears to be included simply to offer contrasting advice to Placebo, and to be more detached and rational. In reality, his opinion is warped by his own experience of unhappy marriage (lines 332–33), and he seems to function as a mouthpiece for the Merchant's own views (see lines 1–4 in 'The Merchant's Prologue'). As with Placebo, Chaucer gives the impression of a rounded character, because by line 443 Justinus has lost all patience with January's folly, and becomes extremely sarcastic. His final action is to leave January to his fate by helping Placebo to arrange the hasty marriage (lines 479–83).

Pluto and Proserpine

These two figures derive from classical mythology. Proserpine was a daughter of Jupiter, king of the gods, and Ceres, the goddess of corn and agriculture. While gathering flowers in the vale of Enna in Sicily, Proserpine was abducted by Pluto and made queen of the underworld. In order to make peace with Ceres, Jupiter gave an order that Proserpine should spend 6 months of the year in the underworld and 6 months above ground. The myth of Proserpine consequently symbolises winter and summer, i.e. January and May.

In 'The Merchant's Tale', Pluto and Proserpine are presented as fairies, like Oberon and Titania in *A Midsummer Night's Dream*, who sometimes visit the mortal world from their home in Faërie. As with Placebo and Justinus, it is remarkable how far Chaucer succeeds in making traditional figures appear as ordinary human beings. Pluto and Proserpine are classical deities, but are portrayed as a normal married couple whose dispute spills over into their treatment of others. Like Oberon and Titania, they meddle with the affairs of humans as a result of their own marital discord.

They are linked to the central **theme** of the tale, the idea of unhappy marriage between unsuitable partners. Although their discord is resolved, it is at the price of the husband's submission — a theme in many of Chaucer's tales. This suits the Merchant's intentions admirably. They are also used to set up the **denouement** of the tale, and their argument serves to postpone that denouement by 100 lines and thus create dramatic suspense within the narrative.

Themes

Marriage

Although 'The Merchant's Tale' is the longest verse story in *The Canterbury Tales*, apart from the Knight's, it is almost exclusively concerned with the theme of marriage. Every part of it (including the digressions) and every character is concerned with marriage, and Chaucer pursues the topic relentlessly. Furthermore, 'The Merchant's Tale' is just one of a linked group of tales on the same subject, which the critic Kittredge has dubbed 'the marriage group' (see pp. 37–39).

Some critics have even attempted to see marriage as a unifying, and perhaps central, theme in *The Canterbury Tales*. There are several reasons for this emphasis:

- Marriage is a fertile subject for stories, particularly for comedy, as there are always grounds for conflict and discord between married couples and lovers.
- A discussion of marriage is a good way of exploring social values and behaviour, including the relative merits and status of men and women. This was as much a topic of debate in the fourteenth century as it is in the twenty-first, and is one of the reasons why Chaucer has remained such a popular writer throughout history.
- Marriage is a religious sacrament with specific promises and bonds between the married parties, so using marriage as a central image is a way of exploring the morality and spirituality of individuals and society.
- Christ's union with the Church on Earth was symbolically seen as a marriage; any human marriage can therefore be judged against the values of Christianity and God's will and providence in a more direct way than may be immediately apparent to the modern reader. This is clearly of importance in a work with as specific a religious context as that of *The Canterbury Tales*.

Remember that attitudes to marriage in the Middle Ages were different from those current today. Marriage was primarily a business or political transaction; it was a means of forming suitable alliances and obtaining security (for a woman) or funds (for a man, through the system of dowries), and for securing inheritance through the production of children. Love was rarely a factor, and romantic love between husband and wife was not merely an irrelevance, it could be actively frowned on as encouraging sin. The Catholic Church (Chaucer wrote a century before the Reformation and Protestantism) taught that there were two reasons for marriage: to beget children, and to avoid the sin of lechery (sex for the latter purpose was known as 'paying one's debt', according to St Paul's teaching in the New Testament. Enjoyment of sex, even between married couples, was held to be sinful to the point of being a mortal sin — lechery. It is no surprise that under such a repressive doctrine, romantic love was largely seen as independent of marriage, and often in opposition to it. Courtly love, in which the noble lover would worship his lady, offered a legitimate manifestation of romantic sentiments without threatening the stability of Christian society.

Chaucer's treatment of marriage in *The Canterbury Tales* can be seen as an important and liberal critique of the institution as it existed in his time. He is invariably sympathetic to women, and often presents them as repressed partners in contracts over which they have no control.

The unsuitability of the marriage

The marriage between January and May is unsuitable on both practical and symbolic grounds.

Practical considerations

The significant issue is the age discrepancy. January is 60, which in medieval terms is very old; May's exact age is not specified, but she must be under 20 to meet January's stipulations (lines 205 and 414). Although a disparity in age is not an automatic barrier to a successful marriage, it becomes one here because of the attitudes of the partners.

Half the time January treats May as a chattel, something he has purchased. This is in keeping with the conventional view of marriage in the Middle Ages, but (unlike the medieval attitude), January is not primarily concerned about May's status or wealth. Instead he is obsessed with the idea of possessing a young and beautiful woman entirely for himself, and he is consumed by lust, which he is unable to fulfil. His claim that they can do no sin because they are married (lines 626–28) would be contested by many medieval theologians, and Chaucer makes it obvious that he is guilty of the mortal sin of lechery.

We do not learn May's view of the marriage for the first half of the tale; presumably this is a standard medieval arranged marriage, in which the bride's wishes were usually irrelevant. From the wedding night onwards, however, she becomes increasingly dissatisfied and independent, and begins to arrange matters in her own interests.

Symbolic reasons

The central symbolism surrounds their names. The month of January represents mid-winter, the harshest and bleakest time of the year for a medieval audience. Significantly, it is a time when nature is 'dead' and nothing grows or is fertile; January's boasts about his virility in lines 246–54, when he compares himself to an evergreen laurel, are exposed as false on his wedding night. May, however, is the month when spring is in full bloom, with all the promise of fecundity and richness of the growing year. It would carry extra significance for a medieval audience, for whom it represented survival after another winter; *The Canterbury Tales* opens in April with exactly this kind of celebration of rebirth and renewal.

The symbolic contrast between January and May means that their marriage is impossible. January describes himself as 'hoor and oold' (line 188), while May is compared to the month she is named after (line 536).

The Merchant's portrayal of the marriage

The Merchant is responding to the representation of marriage given in 'The Clerk's Tale', where the wife is portrayed as passive and subservient. 'The Merchant's Prologue' has revealed him as an unhappily married man, and so he wishes to show marriage in as poor a light as possible. Every part of the tale is designed to reinforce the Merchant's bitterness: the **ironic** digression in lines 55–180, the strictures of Justinus, the quarrel between Pluto and Proserpine, as well as the central narrative. The depth of January's folly is revealed by his proclamation that marriage is 'paradis' (line 53), and his fear that he may forfeit his place in heaven because of his bliss on Earth (lines 425–40).

Chaucer's view of marriage

Chaucer manifestly has a separate purpose from the Merchant. The Merchant's view of marriage is only one contribution to an ongoing debate in *The Canterbury Tales*. Note that it is not marriage itself that is condemned in 'The Merchant's Tale', only unsuitable instances of it. The fact that the Merchant, Justinus and Pluto all have marital difficulties is simply recognition that many marriages have problems. Chaucer seems to express a view of marriage that a modern audience would tend to share — that people should be careful in their choice of partners, and patient in the treatment of their spouses.

Women

It is possible to view 'The Merchant's Tale' as both pro- and anti-feminist. The tale contains strong female characters who refuse to be subservient and who take control of their own destinies. May is no meekly compliant wife; she condemns January's attempts at lovemaking (line 642) and engineers the assignation with Damyan. The epithet 'fresshe' is frequently used of her (e.g. lines 570, 610, 670, 674), and the word suggests her character as well as her symbolic function; she is active and hard for January to restrain. Proserpine also contends with her husband, and gains ascendancy over him when she aids May in deceiving January. In this sense, the tale can be seen as celebrating women's independence and ability to fight their own corner; but it can equally be taken as showing women to be scheming and deceitful, defying their husbands and failing to keep their proper place. Your judgement will partly depend on whether you consider the tale from a modern or a medieval viewpoint.

Folly

January's folly is at the heart of the tale, but the conduct of other characters can

be criticised as well. May is foolish to agree to such an unsuitable marriage (although admittedly she probably had no choice); Justinus realises his folly in expecting his advice to have any effect; Pluto is foolish in expecting to be able to overrule Proserpine. None of the characters emerge with much credit from the tale, and that is part of its humour.

Social conventions

The tale is a study of the consequences of unrealistic expectations, but the situation it describes must have been quite common in the Middle Ages, when romance and marriage were largely separate. Older, richer men such as January must have been able to choose young wives who could be expected to provide them children, and maybe a worthwhile dowry. Human nature, however, would ensure that other relationships were likely, and adultery must have been as attractive for women as it was for men. Shakespeare's Romeo and Juliet are startling in placing romantic love before social convention; 'The Merchant's Tale' presents a much more realistic account of marriage and its surrounding conventions in the Middle Ages.

Love

It is notable that in a tale about marriage, love is not a theme. There is no love between January and May, only sexual obsession on his side and revulsion on hers. Nor is there genuine love between May and Damyan; he is conventionally lovesick with longing for her, and she proclaims love for him (lines 771–72), but their relationship is solely physical when it occurs.

Humour

'The Merchant's Tale' is a satire in that it holds up examples of folly for ridicule. As part of this mockery, Chaucer makes use of a range of comic devices, and although there is considerable overlap it is worth trying to define and distinguish various kinds.

Situational humour

January's desire to marry

January has managed to live to the age of 60 without marrying, but indulging his 'bodily delit' (line 37). His sudden desire to marry seems to be prompted by a need for security in old age, but he has no intention of curbing his amorous instincts. He may genuinely want an heir, but he has left the matter too late, hence the ridiculous haste with which the whole business is conducted.

January's choice of wife

His choice is absurd, as he desires a pretty young woman as if he were still a virile young man. Being a rich knight, he can afford to acquire the object of his desire, but he doesn't appreciate the likely consequences of his actions.

January's blindness

January's metaphorical and literal blindness underpin the tale. He is blind to his own situation and the folly of his expectations about marriage; he is blind to the desires and wishes of his young wife. He fails to listen to his friends; he fails to prevent his wife being adulterous. All these situations offer scope for comic treatment.

Satire

The folly of an unsuitable marriage (see pp. 47–48) is Chaucer's primary target for satire, and leads to further targets — the foolishness of an old man, the unscrupulous behaviour of May and Damyan, and the social conventions of medieval society. The purpose of satire is to reveal vices or folly by exposing them to ridicule, and almost everything Chaucer writes has this purpose — he wants his audience to laugh at the topics he presents to them, but also to think seriously about the issues. You will need to do the same, because examination questions frequently direct attention to Chaucer's satiric purpose.

Irony

It is worth stressing the variety and depth of Chaucer's irony. Some examples have immediate local impact (e.g. lines 1126–27), whereas line 386 relates to the entire narrative. You should find your own examples, but a few are given below.

> Love is blind alday... (line 386)

This is the central irony of the tale; January is metaphorically blind throughout; on the only occasion when he can 'see', after Pluto's miraculous restoration of his sight, May persuades him that he is still half-blind.

> How sholde I thanne, that live in swich plesaunce
> As alle wedded men doon with hire wyvys...? (lines 438–39)

An obvious irony from the Merchant; his entire tale exists to disprove this assertion.

> Upon my soule somwhat moste I thinke.   (line 190)

This is subtle. January seems sincere; in a medieval world, where the threat of death is always present, he may even be sincere. But the hollowness of his claim is revealed 15 lines later, when he insists he will only marry a young wife. If he were interested in saving his soul, he would marry a more suitable lady.

> To take a wif it is a glorious thing… (line 56)

The type of irony in this line depends on who is thought to be saying it. If it is the Merchant then it is sarcastic; if it is January then he will be proved wrong.

> 'Allas,' quod he, 'that I ne had heer a knave
> That koude climbe.' (lines 1126–27)

This is obviously comic, as a 'knave' who is an adept climber is indeed present, in the form of Damyan.

> He that misconceyveth, he misdemeth. (line 1198)

This is again subtle. As a proverb it makes complete sense. The irony is that this is the single moment when January has not misconceived — he has realised precisely what is going on (lines 1181–83). May's skill, prompted by Proserpine, is to make him believe that he does not 'see' clearly.

Bawdiness

The most obvious examples of bawdiness are the descriptions of the lovemaking of January (lines 609–45 and 744–54) and Damyan (lines 1140–41).

January's lovemaking is obscene because he is so physically repulsive; it is always described as 'work' (line 630 and 753), signifying its laborious quality and the lack of pleasure associated with it. By contrast, Damyan's efforts are instantaneous (line 1141), though no more romantic.

It is worth noting the Merchant's (or Chaucer's) coy claim in lines 1138–39 that he does not want to offend lady members of the audience by crudeness; this conventional disclaimer merely adds to the comedy.

'The Merchant's Tale' as a fabliau

In the medieval period, fabliaux were short, comic or satirical tales, realistic rather than idealised, and dealing with middle- or lower-class characters rather than the nobility. The setting was normally contemporary, rather than the 'once upon a time' of romances, and the language was usually colloquial and coarse. They were frequently bawdy or obscene, with characters who tended to flout authority and who were admired more often for their cunning than for their morality. A standard theme was the adultery of a repressed wife, usually with a clever or cunning cleric.

Fabliaux became popular in France in the twelfth and thirteenth centuries, although they were part of the long tradition that lower-class characters were only suitable for comic treatment; lofty themes were reserved for noble characters. This is a tendency that can be observed right back to classical times, and more recently in Shakespeare, where the comic interest in the tragedies is frequently provided by common folk, such as the porter in *Macbeth* or the gravediggers in *Hamlet*.

Chaucer was obviously fond of the fabliau form — its comic potential could be exploited to address serious themes. Although critics do not agree about a precise definition, the tales of the Merchant, the Reeve, the Cook, the Friar, the Summoner, the Miller and the Shipman are normally labelled fabliaux.

'The Miller's Tale' is Chaucer's classic example of the **genre**. It features a foolish husband deceived by a scheming wife. The whole story is bawdy and obscene, with an emphasis on crude bodily functions — farting, defecation and sex — and the language is appropriately coarse.

By comparison, 'The Merchant's Tale' is more refined. It contains the central fabliau theme of the cuckolded husband, deceived by the cunning of his wife and her lover. There is a significant emphasis on the physical process of sexual intercourse, with January's strenuous efforts being contrasted with the abruptness of Damyan. But the tale also includes important departures from the traditional fabliau, to fit the Merchant's relatively refined character and the serious moral purpose of the tale:

- The characters are from the nobility rather than the peasantry (although their behaviour is no different).
- There is no focus on basic bodily functions such as farting. Instead, there is considerable description of January's physical frailty.
- The Merchant does use crude language.
- The Merchant uses a vast array of sources and references, which raises the tone of the story and has the incidental effect of making it almost twice as long as the Miller's.

The tale and its teller

The match between the tale and the teller is an issue throughout *The Canterbury Tales*. Because of the incomplete nature of the project, there is considerable variation in this regard. Some tales are not matched to their narrators at all, for example 'The Nun's Priest's Tale', as the Nun's Priest is left undescribed in 'The General Prologue'. In other cases the match has not been decided; for example in 'The Shipman's Tale' there is evidence that the tale originally had a female narrator. But in some cases the relationship is highly developed. The finest examples are 'The Wife of Bath's Tale' and 'The Pardoner's Tale'; these tales are perfectly matched to their tellers because the Wife and the Pardoner are given an extended prologue to their own tale — in the Wife of Bath's case, her prologue is twice the length of the tale she tells.

'The Merchant's Tale' is not designed specifically for its narrator. It has nothing to do with trade or any of the business that, on the evidence of 'The General Prologue', occupies the Merchant himself. There he is literally an anonymous figure, and the fact that he is married is not mentioned. Nevertheless, Chaucer forges a tale that seems suitable for the Merchant to tell.

The prologue

The information in 'The Merchant's Prologue' is entirely supplementary to the portrait in 'The General Prologue', and if anything contradicts it. 'The General Prologue' gives the reader a picture of a dubious businessman, but one who is so unremarkable that Chaucer the pilgrim claims not to be able to remember his name. There is no mention of a wife, or of any personal characteristics. In 'The Merchant's Prologue' he emerges as a far more distinctive figure, with a voice of his own and a tale to tell, although the single fact we discover is that he is newly married (line 22), to a shrewish and cruel wife (lines 10 and 13). Fanciful readers might suggest that he has come on the pilgrimage to escape her, but there is no textual evidence to support this idea; such a thought reveals the weakness of trying to imagine Chaucer's pilgrims as 'real' human beings.

The tale

The Merchant's tale is entirely consistent with his characterisation in 'The Merchant's Prologue', being an extended complaint about marriage, and has echoes of the Merchant's own manner, as described in 'The General Prologue'

The Merchant is 'sowninge alwey th'encrees of his winning' ('The General Prologue', line 277); he continually boasts about his profits, even though he is later revealed to be in debt. January in 'The Merchant's Tale' behaves in a similar way: he boasts of his young wife and is obsessed by her, but she deceives him. His insistence on the superficial aspects of possessing a 'trophy wife' is shown to be a sham, wholly at odds with the proper nature of Christian marriage.

The subtlety here is that the **analogy** between January and the Merchant is entirely Chaucer's. The Merchant would not intentionally tell a tale exposing the folly of superficiality, since he depends on it for his self-image and his worldly credibility. Although his tale succeeds as a comic representation of the traditional unsuitability of the marriage of age and youth, Chaucer makes it rebound on its teller to reveal the perils of judgements made solely on appearances. Chaucer's purpose is to emphasise this folly by giving a double example of it in the narrator and in the tale he tells. The point is developed further in the Merchant's epilogue, in which the literal-minded Host, Harry Bailly, takes the story at face value, and adds his own conventional complaint against shrewish wives. A similar phenomenon occurs even more subtly in 'The Pardoner's Tale'.

Realism, fantasy and symbol

You should construct your own list of these features. The following are given as a starting point:

Realistic features	Fantastic elements	Symbols
Place (lines 33–34)	Fairies (lines 1013–23)	Names (January, May, Placebo, Justinus)
Descriptive writing (lines 612–13 and 637)	January's blindness (lines 857–59)	January's blindness (lines 857–59)
Old man's lust (lines 538–52)	Formal debates about marriage (lines 1025–1107)	The garden (lines 817–29)
Young woman's disgust (lines 639–42)	Comic denouement (lines 1142–1206)	The pear tree (lines 997–99)
Young woman's unfaithfulness (lines 732–42)		

It is clear that Chaucer is willing to combine different literary forms in a free and inclusive manner. While modern literature often tends to separate works into types or **genres**, Chaucer integrates disparate material at will. Sometimes this is for **satirical** effect, e.g. the contrast between the realism of January's 'slakke skin' (line 637) and his symbolic claim to be evergreen (lines 253–54); sometimes it is thematic, e.g. January is symbolically blind throughout the tale (line 386), and this is emphasised by his entirely unexplained and sudden physical blindness. He then magically regains his sight at the critical moment, only to revert to metaphorical blindness as May persuades him that he is in error. There are some highly symbolic features, especially the garden and the pear tree. The garden is taken from medieval romance (the *Roman de la Rose*), but its parallels with the Garden of Eden are made explicit by the numerous mentions of paradise in the tale, leaving the audience in no doubt that it will be the setting for deception and a 'Fall'. The pear tree traditionally appears in fairy-tales.

The intertwining of these elements is sometimes considerable. Pluto and Proserpine are as naturalistic as any of the other characters in terms of their marital relationship, argument and reconciliation; yet they are classical deities presented as fairies, who quote biblical authorities in the course of their realistic dialogue. You should think of and examine as many examples as possible.

The use of authorities

The use of 'auctoritees' (authorities) is one of the most characteristic and important parts of medieval literature. Using the notes in your edition of the text, you should examine the range of authorities quoted within 'The Merchant's Tale'. These include:

- the Bible — throughout the tale, but especially lines 150–62
- Theophrastus — line 82
- Albertano and Deschamps (these two are not directly named) — lines 144–49
- Seneca — lines 164 and 311
- Cato — line 165
- the Wife of Bath — line 473
- Martianus Capella — line 520
- Constantine Afer — line 598
- Ovid — line 913
- Claudian — line 1020

There are also references to:

- Fortune — lines 102 and 845
- folk sayings — lines 206 and 212
- classical legend — line 504
- Venus — lines 511 and 565
- astronomy — line 673
- the *Roman de la Rose* — line 820
- Argus — line 899

Examination of the reliance on such authorities leads to several conclusions, which are listed below.

(1) Medieval respect for 'auctoritees' is richly confirmed in this tale. Chaucer uses a wide variety of sources to support and deepen the themes of 'The Merchant's Tale', with all the characters citing authorities in order to support their points of view.

(2) The emphasis on authority underlines the lack of value assigned to originality for its own sake.

(3) Biblical authorities are pre-eminent. It is notable that even Pluto and Proserpine, classical deities masquerading as fairies, use scripture to support their arguments. A key example is lines 926–37, where January bizarrely appropriates the Song of Solomon for his own purposes. You should also examine lines 150–62 in detail.

(4) Chaucer's own erudition is demonstrated in abundance. The range of sources and the types of literature with which he was evidently familiar should be stressed: Chaucer was a highly educated and well-read man.

(5) The Merchant would not share Chaucer's level of learning, and the device of the pilgrim narrator is simply a technique. Chaucer does not expect his audience to believe that a merchant is truly telling the story.

(6) A particular point of interest is the reference to the Wife of Bath in line 473. Technically, this line is spoken by Justinus; the reader can see it either as a simple error on Chaucer's part, assigning knowledge of one fictional character to another fictional character within the same work, or as a comment on the lack of verisimilitude in Chaucer's writing: a medieval audience might have had no difficulty in accepting this surreal moment of narrative technique.

(7) A rare exception to the general use of authorities occurs at line 446, where Justinus is so angry that he speaks from the heart. This is an unusual instance of a very realistic piece of writing by Chaucer, and can help explain the immediate appeal of his work for modern readers.

Chaucer's narrative technique

'The Merchant's Tale' is not entirely original. The folk tale of the enchanted pear tree emerges in various guises. Other elements of the story can also be traced to sources with which Chaucer would have been familiar. However, no single model for the story is known, so it seems likely that Chaucer adapted a range of elements to create the effect he wanted. This is in keeping with much of *The Canterbury Tales*, and it is worth comparing Chaucer and Shakespeare in this regard; both writers adapted existing stories and material to suit their own purposes. This was the standard practice of their times, when retelling old stories was viewed as a more worthy pursuit than inventing new ones.

As it stands, 'The Merchant's Tale' can certainly be viewed as entirely Chaucer's creation, and the ways in which he develops the **narrative** are worth studying. Note that at 1,174 lines the tale is the second longest in *The Canterbury Tales*.

Pace

This is not an action story; it is chiefly concerned with developing the **themes** of the blindness of dotage and the perils of unsuitable marriage, hence digressions like that of lines 55–180, which is of such length that it is as important as the narrative it interrupts. Similarly, the contributions of Placebo and Justinus are part of the story, but serve a larger purpose outside it as contributions to the debate on marriage. The intrusion of Pluto and Proserpine does the same, albeit it in a more complex fashion, but in this case it has a direct narrative function in delaying the **denouement** of the tale while also contributing to it.

The main action sequence, when it finally arrives in line 1108, is a masterpiece of compression and swift action. The arrival at the pear tree, the sex, the quick-fire **dialogue** between January and May when he recovers his sight, are all deftly and amusingly dovetailed. Chaucer's ability to handle an episode in this way confirms that the earlier languorousness of the tale is no accident, but a deliberate lingering on **thematic** developments that the author regards as of equal or greater significance to the story. Elsewhere, Chaucer makes use of **rhetorical** flourishes, such as direct address and **apostrophe**, to heighten the mock-seriousness of the situation (e.g. lines 571–82).

'Sodeynly'

The word 'sodeynly' is used four times in the tale, most notably in line 859. The suddenness of many of the instances in the story emphasises its lack of realism. Chaucer is not concerned with creating a naturalistic **narrative**; instead, he wishes to highlight particular moments and events. Even where the word 'sodeynly' is not used, events often have an unexplained immediacy, such as Damyan's sickness and recovery.

Speech and dialogue

Approximately 40% of the tale is speech and dialogue, and there are also occasional asides and characters' thoughts. The seven speakers are divided as follows:

January	192 lines
May	65 lines
Damyan	2 lines
Placebo	41 lines
Justinus	75 lines
Pluto	32 lines
Proserpine	51 lines

Despite the restriction of the rhyming couplet form, Chaucer's command of colloquial dialogue is one of his most striking and well-known attributes. He creates both extended speeches and realistic dialogue with equal ease. The following is of particular note:

- Speech often aids characterisation (e.g. lines 203–10 and 346–53).
- Colloquialisms add to the realism of speech and situations (e.g. lines 354–55 and 1052–55).
- Dialogue can forcefully drive the narrative (e.g. lines 1126–33 and 1154–208).

Literary terms and concepts

Assessment Objective 1 requires 'insight appropriate to literary study, using appropriate terminology'. A knowledge of literary terms is therefore essential for A-level literature students, and allows responses to texts to be worded precisely and concisely. The terms and concepts below have been selected for their relevance to the study of 'The Merchant's Prologue and Tale'.

allegory	extended metaphor which veils a moral, religious or political underlying meaning
alliteration	repetition of initial letter or sound in adjacent words to create an atmospheric or onomatopoeic effect, e.g. 'maken melodye' ('The Merchant's Tale', line 828)
ambiguity	capacity of words to have two meanings in the context as a device for enriching meaning
analogy	perception of similarity between two things
apostrophe	direct address to a divinity, object or abstract concept, such as Freedom
archetype	original model used as recurrent symbol, e.g. the Garden of Eden
assonance	repetition of vowel sound in words in close proximity
bathos	sudden change of register from the sublime to the ridiculous
bawdy	lewd; with coarse, humorous references to sex
blazon	device in medieval poetry whereby a woman's body is described and celebrated in close detail
caricature	exaggerated and ridiculous portrayal of a person built around a specific physical or personality trait, e.g. the sycophancy of Placebo
characterisation	means by which fictional characters are personified and made distinctive
climax	moment of intensity to which a series of events has been leading
colloquial	informal language of conversational speech
contextuality	historical, social and cultural background of a text
couplet	two consecutive lines of poetry which are paired in rhyme
courtly love	in the Middle Ages a code governing the behaviour of aristocratic lovers, with a subservient lover adoring an idealised woman
criticism	evaluation of literary text or other artistic work

denouement	unfolding of the final stages of a plot, when all is revealed
dialogue	direct speech of characters engaged in conversation
didactic	with the intention of teaching the reader and instilling moral values
elements	earth, air, fire, water, of which it was believed in the Middle Ages that the universe was composed, with corresponding humours to explain human temperament
empathy	identifying with a character in a literary work
end-stopped	line of poetry which ends with some form of punctuation, creating a pause
enjamb(e)ment	run-on instead of end-stopped line of poetry, usually to reflect meaning
epicurean	devoted to luxury and self-indulgence
epithet	recurring characteristic adjective affixed to a name, e.g. 'olde Januarie' (line 744), 'fresshe May' (line 674)
fabliau	short medieval tale in rhyme, of a coarsely comic and satirical nature
farce	improbable and absurd dramatic events to excite laughter
figurative	imagery; non-literal use of language
genre	type or form of writing with identifiable characteristics, e.g. fairy tale, fabliau
heroic couplet	iambic pentameter rhymed in pairs; traditional form of classical epic poetry and the form used in 'The Merchant's Tale'
humours	four bodily fluids produced by different organs and related to one of the elements, an excess of which caused particular temperaments: yellow bile (anger), blood (happiness), phlegm (calmness), black bile (melancholy)
iambic pentameter	five feet of iambs, i.e. unstressed/stressed alternating syllables
imagery	descriptive language appealing to the senses; imagery may be sustained or recurring throughout texts, usually in the form of simile or metaphor

irony	a discrepancy between the actual and implied meaning of language; or an amusing or cruel reversal of an outcome expected, intended or deserved; situation in which one is mocked by fate or the facts
juxtaposition	placing side by side for (ironic) contrast of interpretation
legend	story about historical figures which exaggerates their qualities or feats
metaphor	suppressed comparison implied not stated, e.g. when the Merchant describes marriage in his tale: 'in this world it is a paradis' (line 53)
metre	regular series of stressed and unstressed syllables in a line of poetry
myth	fiction involving supernatural beings which explains natural and social phenomena and embodies traditional and popular ideas
narrative	connected and usually chronological series of events that form a story
parody	imitation and exaggeration of style for purpose of humour and ridicule
pathos	evocation of pity by a situation of suffering and helplessness
plot	cause-and-effect sequence of events caused by characters' actions
register	level of formality of expression
rhetoric	art of persuasion using emotive language and stylistic devices, e.g. triple structures, rhetorical questions
rhyme	repetition of final vowel sound in words at the end of lines of poetry
rhythm	pace and sound pattern of writing, created by metre, vowel length, syntax and punctuation
romance	story of love and heroism, deriving from medieval court life and fairy tale
satire	exposing vice or foolishness of a person or institution to ridicule
scansion	system of notation for marking stressed (/) and unstressed (~) syllables in a line of metrical verse

seven deadly sins	according to the medieval Catholic Church, the following sins were mortal and led straight to Hell: pride, envy, anger, sloth, avarice, gluttony, lust
simile	comparison introduced by 'as' or 'like', e.g. 'They live but as a brid or as a beest' (line 69)
stereotype	category of person with typical characteristics, often used for mockery
syntax	arrangement of grammar and word order in sentence construction
theme	abstract idea or issue explored in a text
tone	emotional aspect of the voice of a text, e.g. 'Justinus, which that hated his folye' (line 443), which expresses the Merchant's cynicism
wit	intelligent verbal humour

Questions & Answers

LITERATURE

Essay questions, specimen plans and notes

This section includes a range of essay questions on 'The Merchant's Prologue and Tale', together with examining board material to help you understand what the examiners are looking for. Examinations may be of the 'open book' variety, where you are permitted to take a copy of the text (normally with your own annotations) into the examination, or of the 'closed book' variety, where you are not permitted the text in the examination. Note that A-level students are expected to use accurate quotations to support points, so for a closed book examination you will need to learn as many quotations as you are likely to need. Quotations from Chaucer should always be given in the original Middle English, not in modernised form or paraphrase.

Passage-based questions: prescribed

A question of this type will direct you to a particular extract from the text. It will ask a specific question about the passage, but also ask you to place the extract in the context of the whole text. Examiners advise that a substantial portion (up to 60%) of responses to passage-based questions should refer to the rest of the work being studied. Answers that only deal with the specified extract are likely to be heavily penalised. Focus closely on the passage(s) but also relate their content and/or language to elsewhere in the text, backwards and forwards, and link your comments to the overall themes and/or structure of the text. Start by placing the passage in its context and summarising the situation. Include references to character, event, theme and language, and ask how the episode modifies or adds to our understanding so far, and how typical it is of the work as a whole.

1 'The Merchant's Prologue and Tale' is set in a particular period and place, but it is full of generalisations about human nature.' Explore Chaucer's craft in the light of this statement. You should commence your answer with a consideration of lines 33–80, the opening passage of the tale.

Possible ideas to include in a plan
- medieval setting
- medieval/Christian attitudes to marriage
- medieval attitudes to age
- expectations of knightly behaviour
- the eternal issue of 'the age gap'
- behaviour of young people
- attitudes to sex

- modern attitudes to marriage
- self-delusion
- unwillingness to listen to advice

Edexcel grade description: grade A

Students demonstrate a comprehensive, detailed knowledge and understanding of a wide range of literary texts from the past to the present, and of the critical concepts associated with literary study. Their discussion of texts shows depth, independence and insight in response to the tasks set, and they analyse and evaluate the ways in which form, structure and language shape meanings. Where appropriate, students identify the influence on texts of the cultural and historical contexts in which they were written. They are able to make significant and productive comparisons between texts which enhance and extend their readings, and are sensitive to the scope of their own and others' interpretations of texts. Their material is well organised and presented, making effective use of textual evidence in support of arguments. Written expression is fluent, well-structured, accurate and precise, and shows confident grasp of appropriate terminology.

Further questions

2 Reread lines 425–76. How do you view January and Justinus here and what is the importance of this discussion to the tale as a whole?

3 Turn to the ending of 'The Merchant's Tale', beginning at line 1108. How satisfactory an ending do you consider this to be, bearing in mind all that has gone before in the tale?

4 Look again at the discussion between Pluto and Proserpine (lines 1022–107). What do you find of interest in this discussion and what is the significance of the appearance of Pluto and Proserpine at this point in the tale?

5 In what ways does the prologue to 'The Merchant's Tale' contribute to the irony in the tale itself?

6 Turn to the debate between Placebo and Justinus (lines 266–353). Compare these two speeches both in the arguments that are used and in the ways in which they reveal something of the personalities of the speakers. Explain the place of this debate in the context of the tale overall.

Passage-based questions: selected

The advice given above for set passages should be followed here too, with the advantage that you can select your own material as a focus for your essay. Careful selection of passages is crucial to ensure the relevance and success of the essay. The choice of extract is obviously critical here; a well-chosen extract can do half your work for you, while a poorly chosen one can mean a struggle to answer the question adequately. The passages you like or are most familiar with are not necessarily the most appropriate for a particular title. Try to choose passages covering a range of characters, attitudes or moods if this is possible and relevant to the question. You should practise this type of question frequently prior to the examination.

1 **'Chaucer looks at the society of his day with a gentle humour.' To what extent do you agree with this statement? You will need to refer to at least *two* extracts of your choice (each approximately 50 lines). (Source: Edexcel Support Material)**

Possible ideas to include in a plan

- key words are satire and irony
- more forceful than 'gentle' humour
- key target is marriage
- folly of January
- disloyalty of May
- disloyalty of Damyan
- January's refusal to listen to advice
- self-interest of Placebo and Justinus
- many of these are equally modern topics, not just medieval

Further questions

2 Would it be fair to describe 'The Merchant's Tale' as 'a morally shabby story'? You will need to refer to at least *two* extracts of your choice (each approximately 50 lines). (Source: Edexcel support material)

3 Do you have any sympathy with January in 'The Merchant's Tale'? You will need to refer to at least *two* extracts of your choice (each approximately 50 lines).

4 'The tale told by the Merchant is rich in ironic effects.' Consider 'The Merchant's Tale' in the light of this comment. You will need to refer to at least *two* extracts of your choice (each approximately 50 lines).

5 'The Merchant's Tale' has been described as 'setting personal and materialistic gain against spiritual values'. How helpful do you find this description to your understanding of the tale and its effects? You will need to refer to at least *two* extracts of your choice (each approximately 50 lines).

Whole-text questions

Underline the key words in the question and ensure that you address them thoroughly. Look out for questions asking you 'how' Chaucer achieves effects or 'why' he includes particular details. Unless the question is given in bullet points the structure of the essay is entirely your responsibility, and you should take special care in planning your work before you start.

1 One critic has observed that 'Chaucer enhances the tale by setting it within the context of the Merchant's own personality and experience'. How important do you

consider Chaucer's characterisation of the Merchant to the effect of the prologue and tale as a whole?

Possible ideas to include in a plan

- focus on the Merchant's prologue for his attitude to marriage
- refer to the Merchant's boastfulness in 'The General Prologue'
- examine how these aspects deepen the irony of the tale
- examine digression on marriage (lines 55–180) and whether this is the Merchant's voice or January's
- emphasis on January's blindness about May
- comedy of the tale remains despite the Merchant's bitterness

OCR mark description

Answers that are penetrating and original will show:

AO1   Assured presentation of cogent arguments, using appropriate terminology.

AO2ii   Sophisticated understanding of poetry in general and of Chaucer's verse in particular, exploring and commenting in depth on characterisation in the prologue and tale, making accurate and relevant cross-reference to other texts and writers as appropriate.

AO3   Insight into how Chaucer achieves complex effects of characterisation and irony through verse, not only in description but also by the use of other poetic methods.

AO4   Independent opinions and judgements formed by their own reading of the poem, evaluating the helpfulness of the interpretation offered and venturing alternative suggestions.

AO5ii   A real appreciation of the influence of social, cultural, economic and historical perspectives on their reading of the verse, noting characteristic attitudes of the context in which the poem is set and of the times in which it was written, and commenting on the possible tension between these and their own twentieth-century and other perspectives.

Further questions

2 'The Merchant presents a thoroughly cynical view of women and marriage.' How far do you consider such a statement to be an accurate description of 'The Merchant's Tale'?

3 How far do you agree that in 'The Merchant's Tale' Chaucer does not judge wickedness but is simply amused by it?

4 'Chaucer does not much care for the materialistic elements in society.' By close reference to the portrait of the Merchant and the way he tells his tale, say how far you agree with this view.

5 Which do you think is the most admirable or least admirable of the characters in 'The Merchant's Tale'? How does their portrait relate to the moral values of the medieval world?

6 Discuss the effects of the way Chaucer introduces the character of January to the reader. Look closely at the effects of language, descriptive detail and imagery in creating an impression.

Practice questions

These questions are an additional resource. They are designed to be used as practice at any stage of your study of the text. Some are suitable for brief answers as well as more extended essays.

1 Is the essential tone of 'The Merchant's Prologue and Tale' morally serious or comic?

2 How far can Damyan be regarded as a courtly lover and how far as simply 'the lechour, in the tree' (line 1045)?

3 Can 'The Merchant's Tale' be viewed as antifeminist?

4 Chaucer's irony is not always kindly and tolerant. Choose two passages in 'The Merchant's Tale' where you think he conveys strong disapproval and show how he achieves this effect.

5 'Self-deception is the most important theme in the 'The Merchant's Tale'.' How far do you agree with this reading of the text?

6 Discuss the symbolic implications of the fruit imagery in the 'The Merchant's Tale'.

7 Discuss the symbolic implications of the references to blindness in the 'The Merchant's Tale'.

Sample essays

Below are two sample student essays of different types, both falling within the top mark band. You can judge them against the Assessment Objectives for this text for your exam board and decide on the mark you think each deserves, and why. You will be able to see ways in which each could be improved in terms of content, style and accuracy.

Sample essay 1: passage based

'Modern readers like to think of Chaucer as supremely a comic writer, whereas his contemporaries praised him for his seriousness.' What is your response to these two views? You will need to refer to at least two extracts of your choice (each approximately 50 lines).

I agree that Chaucer is obviously a comic writer, but his underlying seriousness is clear as well, even to a modern reader. I imagine that his original audience would have enjoyed the comic moments just as much as we do, so I don't think the reactions of modern and medieval audiences are very far apart.

To prove my point I will focus on two passages – lines 1126–77, which are near the end, where January catches his wife with Damyan up the tree, and a much earlier passage (lines 365–421), where January is fantasising about the kind of wife he would like.

I will start with the blatant comedy of 'The Merchant's Tale'. There is the obvious humour of January having his sight restored just when the two lovers are up the tree – he 'saugh that Damyan his wyf had dressed/In swich manere it may nay been expressed' – and his appalled reaction to this. The comedy is heightened because May is unconcerned, and immediately has the excuse that for her to 'strugle with a man upon a tree' was the best way to cure January's blindness. The word 'strugle' is particularly funny, and even January 'sees' the absurdity – '"Strugle," quod he, "ye algate in it wente."' The comedy continues as May, prompted by her own wit and by Proserpine, is able to persuade him against the evidence of his own eyes.

There is also more subtle comedy here, based on Chaucer's irony, which I think would be appreciated by both medieval and modern audiences. At the beginning of this extract, January laments the absence of 'a knave/That koude climbe'. I don't think anybody can fail to see how funny this is. A climbing knave is indeed present, and is already in the tree, waiting for his lover, who actually asks January's help to 'give her a leg up': 'So I my foot mighte sette upon youre bak.'

This is all highly amusing, but in the context of the whole tale Chaucer is making a very serious point, and the irony is based on January's 'blindness', which is much more moral than physical. I believe that is why January becomes blind so suddenly: 'this noble Januarie free…Is woxen blind, and that al sodeynly.' I think Chaucer is being sarcastic when he calls January 'noble' and 'free' (generous) because he is neither of those things. He has been metaphorically blind all through the tale: 'For love is blind alday.'

In the early part of the tale January suddenly decides to get married, but it is obvious from the start that he has a totally unrealistic attitude: 'For wedlock is so esy and so clene,/That in this world it is a paradis.' A medieval audience would have been instantly aware of the danger lurking in an earthly paradise, but I don't think this is a difficult concept for modern audiences either. The serious point is that an improper marriage is no marriage at all, and is bound to fail. When we see January imagining what marriage will be like, we know what's going to happen. Pride comes before a fall, says the proverb, and the medieval sin of pride is at the root of January's problems. He doesn't look at the reality.

Instead, in my second extract, he indulges in 'Heigh fantasye and curious bisynesse' when he imagines what kind of woman he might marry. The fatal line gives his decision to 'chees hire of his owene auctoritee'. This may sound innocent to a modern reader, but a member of Chaucer's audience would immediately realise that January is setting himself up as an authority instead of listening to others (including his friends). The earlier reference to paradise, added to this, makes it obvious that he is in grave danger when he imagines:

Hir wise governaunce, hir gentillesse,
Hir wommanly beringe, and hire sadnesse.

I think this combines comedy and seriousness. January is being silly; he is deceiving himself, and he is going to be deceived by his wife. It is also important that it is the Merchant who is telling the story, because he knows how unhappy an unsuitable marriage can be: 'I have a wyf, the worste that may be.' January's choice of May – winter against spring – is absurd. 'This was his fantasye' – the Merchant knows it, Chaucer knows it, and we know it too. The entertainment lies in seeing how deeply January is deceived, and how ingeniously May deceives him. He regards himself as being 'as grene/As laurer', but when he gets to bed 'The slakke skin aboute his nekke shaketh'.

What has happened is that January is living a life of illusion, and reality catches up on him. His pretty young wife naturally turns to a lusty young lover, Damyan, and they outwit him. I think it is very important for the comedy that we don't sympathise with any of the characters, but particularly January. He's deliberately made out to be excessive, so that we enjoy watching him being fooled. His lovemaking is horrible – 'Thus laboureth he til that the day gan dawe' – and his jealousy is intolerable – 'That hadde an hand upon hire everemo'. At the same time serious points are being made about what is reasonable and appropriate behaviour for civilised people. January is supposed to be a respectable elderly knight, and should know better. We can hardly blame May, for whom it's an arranged marriage, and Damyan merely takes his opportunity where he finds it. Nobody emerges with credit, but I am clear that the fault lies with January.

In conclusion, I firmly believe that the tale offers the same pleasures to a modern and a medieval audience. We laugh at the foolish antics of these people, but we don't miss the serious points that Chaucer is making.

Sample essay 2: whole text

'Its irony makes all the laughter uneasy and slightly strained.' How far do you agree with this comment on 'The Merchant's Prologue and Tale'?

Irony is Chaucer's characteristic mode. He makes sure that it is the dominant mode of 'The Merchant's Tale' by giving us the Merchant's prologue, in which the Merchant identifies himself as a recently married man ('Thise monthes two, and moore nat') whose wife is 'the worste that may be'. The Merchant therefore means his tale to be ironic, and a typical example of medieval misogyny – it is meant to show the foolishness of old men and the treachery of women, and nobody's behaviour is to be admired. He means us to laugh, but he wants it to be bitter laughter.

Chaucer's own purpose is more complex. He wants the reader to take a more humane view, a more understanding view, of human motivation and behaviour. It is easy to mock January – the Merchant immediately refers to 'thise fooles' at the beginning of the tale. His belief in his own potency is laughable ('Myn herte and alle my lymes been as grene/As laurer'), especially when compared with the reality of his 'slakke skin'. His attempt to prevent May from straying, by holding her hand at all times, is grotesque, and leads to all the obvious ironies at the end of the tale when she deceives him, and actually stands on his back to do so ('Thanne sholde I climbe wel ynogh…So I my foot mighte sette upon youre bak'). But Chaucer portrays a more complex figure than just a foolish old man.

Even the Merchant is ambivalent about January's motives – 'Were it for hoolinesse or for dotage' – and January's own explanation contains at least partial truth: 'I have my body folily despended'. He wants to redeem his life before he dies, and he wants an heir to avoid his lands falling 'In straunge hand'. A young wife could both reconcile him to God and maintain his bloodline. However, he cannot resist the temptations of lust, and his insistence on a young bride leads to his downfall. The reader laughs at January, but understands him too; he is a human figure, motivated by conflicting human impulses.

His blindness, caused by this confusion, is a subject of irony and comedy which Chaucer richly explores. All the time January can see he is metaphorically blind, 'For love is blind alday, and may nat see.' His sudden physical blindness is thus just a metaphorical enactment of what is already true. The irony is that the only time when he does see clearly ('Struggle…ye algate in it wente'), May manages to convince him that he is still blind ('Ye han som glimsing, and no parfit sighte'). The reader enjoys the irony, but there is no malice in the laughter; January may be blind, but he has also been tricked.

The reader also laughs more easily because January is not the only character in the tale to suffer. May has her moment of passion, but at the end of the tale January leads her back to the house. Damyan too has his moment, but is then dismissed from the narrative without a word. Pluto and Proserpine bicker like any married couple, and even Justinus, that apparently righteous moral arbiter, is revealed as being prejudiced because of his own unhappy marriage ('I have wept many a teere/Ful prively, sin I have had a wyf').

Much of the comedy in the tale is not designed to be 'strained'. It is designed to be genuinely funny, more like a sit-com than a tragicomedy. January's boast of his sexual prowess – 'Al my corage, it is so sharp and keene' – and May's terse judgement of it – 'She preyseth nat his pleying worth a bene' – are frankly funny, as is the irony of January's lament in the garden: 'Allas…that I ne had heer a knave/That koude climbe'. Similarly, the emptiness of Placebo's advice ('I holde youre owene conseil is the beste') and the bitterness of Justinus ('Paraunter she may be youre purgatorie') are closely observed examples of typical human responses – in their own way they are as blind as January. The henpecked Pluto who cannot contest his wife's arguments ('I yeve it up') and the scolding Proserpine ('Hir answere shal she have, I undertake') are all part of the comedy, which leads the reader to smile, not to wince.

There is little doubt that the Merchant wants the audience's laughter to be strained; out of his own bitterness ('Weping and wailing, care and oother sorwe') he wants his audience to laugh uneasily at the extent of human folly. Chaucer, less grudgingly, wants the laughter to be the easy, shared laughter of common humanity. The characters in the tale are foolish, of course, but they are no more foolish than any of us, and we are no more foolish than them. Everybody has conflicting motives for their behaviour, everybody behaves badly or selfishly as circumstances dictate. We can laugh at our own follies without always berating ourselves for them, and this is what Chaucer invites us to do.

Further study

Complete editions

The standard edition is still F. N. Robinson's *The Works of Geoffrey Chaucer* (2nd edn), Oxford University Press (1957).

Larry D. Benson's 1988 edition of *The Riverside Chaucer* (Oxford University Press) is the best complete edition.

Modernised versions

Strictly speaking, it is wrong to use the word translation for Chaucer, as his work (like Shakespeare's) is written in English, albeit Middle English. These are really modernisations, but the word translation is often used.

The best known are the verse renderings by Nevill Coghill (Penguin) and David Wright (Oxford World's Classics). While these give a flavour of Chaucer for the non-specialist, a prose version is more suitable for studying, because it allows direct comparison with the original text. The recommended work is David Wright's prose modernisation of *The Canterbury Tales* (Fontana, 1996). Unfortunately, this omits the 'Tale of Melibee' and 'The Parson's Tale', but is otherwise the best way to read the complete *Tales*.

Readings

The easiest way to hear Chaucer's work read aloud is via the internet; there are a number of sites that offer extracts or complete tales, and some give pronunciation guides too. See the section on internet resources below. Libraries may have cassette tape or audio CD versions, e.g. the Penguin Audiobook version.

Background reading

There is a daunting number of books on Chaucer available; your school and local library will have a selection. It is worth looking out for the following:

Brewer, D. (1996) *Chaucer and His World*, Eyre Methuen. This is an excellent visual and biographical account of Chaucer. Derek Brewer has written and edited a number of accessible books on Chaucer.

Burrow, J. (1982) *Medieval Writers and Their Work: Middle English Literature and its Background 1100–1500*, Oxford University Press. This study places Chaucer in his literary context.

Rowland, B. (ed.) (1979) *Companion to Chaucer Studies*, Oxford University Press. This contains excellent essays on Chaucer and his background.

The internet

The internet is a marvellous source of material on Chaucer, because it permits the use of illustrations and sound in a way that not even the best books can match. There is also an enormous quantity of up-to-date material available, ranging from student guides to academic studies. A good search engine (Google is recommended) and the willingness to spend some time exploring will reveal considerable riches, and often unexpected and useful insights into all aspects of Chaucer's works, period and culture. Try the following starting points:

- www.unc.edu/depts/chaucer/index.html is the *Chaucer Metapage*, designed to offer links to many aspects of Chaucer.
- http://hosting.uaa.alaska.edu/afdtk/etc_genprol.htm contains *The Electronic Canterbury Tales* and a wealth of other information.
- www.luminarium.org/medlit/chaucer.htm is a good introduction to Chaucer.
- http://cla.calpoly.edu/~dschwart/engl512/gp.html has links to useful background material.
- www.mathomtrove.org/canterbury/links.htm is an excellent page of links to material on Chaucer and on the medieval background.
- www.courses.fas.harvard.edu/~chaucer/index.html includes an interactive guide to Chaucer's pronunciation, grammar and vocabulary, and interlinear modernisations of some of the tales.